HOW TO HIT *the* GROUND RUNNING

A Quick-Start Guide

For Congregations
With New Leadership

NEAL O. MICHELL

A catalog record for this book is available from the Library of Congress
ISBN 0-89869-475-2

Church Publishing Incorporated
445 Fifth Avenue
New York, NY 10016
www.churchpublishing.org
5 4 3 2 1

Table of Contents

A Quick Start Guide to Congregational Development

This book is a guide to pastoral leadership competency. Its key message is that the pastor is the leader of the congregation. It will show the pastor, whether novice or experienced, how to be the leader who develops the congregation. The primary target is the pastor of a pastoral-, transitional-, or program-sized church. Taking the new rector or vicar from a month prior to arrival at a new congregation through the first 18 months, this book will help the rector or vicar to integrate pastoral care, buildings and grounds improvements, stewardship and financial accountability, vestry development, and raising the profile of the congregation in the local community to bring about growth, health, and vitality in the local congregation. It is both toolkit and how-to manual for the pastoral leader.

—Neal Michell

Acknowledgments

I would like to thank the five churches that were both my teachers and my classrooms (all Episcopal churches): Holy Trinity, Carrizo Springs, Texas; St. Timothy's, Cotulla, Texas; St. Barnabas', Fredericksburg, Texas; Church of the Redeemer, Germantown, Tennessee; and St. John's, New Braunfels, Texas.

I've had two primary mentors in congregational development: John Maxwell of Injoy and Canon Kevin Martin of Vital Church Ministries. As you read this book, you will probably recognize many things that they have said or written. My failure to cite them is not an attempt to plagiarize so much as it is a recognition that things that I have learned from them have now become my own. Failure to cite them is more an indication of my faulty memory and a credit to their influence.

My three closest cohorts in ministry are Bishop Jim Stanton, Canon Paul Lambert, and Dean Michael Mills. Further, I have learned a tremendous amount from my rector, Rev. David Roseberry, Canon Keith Brown, and Rev'd Victoria Heard. Partners in ministry to whom I owe an invaluable debt are Frank Carter, John Petry, Bob Gates, Tom Alt, George Gibbons, Hunt Campbell, Hal Warfield, Hylmar Karbach, John Castle, Rob Milbank, Brownie Watkins, and Natalie Michell.

My editor, Johnny Ross, has cleaned up a lot of my long-windedness and made many of my ideas much more coherent and condensed.

And, finally, my wife, Varita, has encouraged me throughout our life and ministry together.

Introduction

How to Use This Book

When I graduated from law school, I had no idea where the courthouse was. I did not know how to issue a subpoena. I did not know how to write a simple deed for the sale of a house. During law school, I was taught how to think like a lawyer, not how to practice law. To learn how to practice law, I had to receive on-the-job training.

Similarly, after I graduated from seminary, I had no idea how to run a vestry meeting. I did not know how to work with a senior warden. I had no clue about leadership development. In seminary, I was taught to think like a theologian and to write theological papers. To learn how to be the leader of a congregation, I had to receive on-the-job training as well.

I know many theologically astute clergy who are not very effective leaders of their congregations. I also know many deeply spiritual people who are not very effective leaders. I know many other people who are very committed to their church, who are nevertheless disappointed in their church involvement. They love their church; they believe that their church has a lot to offer; they believe that their church isn't living up to its potential; and they are convinced that their church could do more than it does. They feel frustrated because they don't really know how to make their church more effective.

This book is aimed toward leaders of congregations, both lay and ordained, who want to see their church reach its God-ordained potential. It is a book about how leaders lead in a congregation to help remove the roadblocks that often stymie a church's natural growth.

Who Should Read This Book?

Basically, two kinds of leaders will benefit from this book.

First is the pastor who has recently been called to serve a congregation. This book will help you lay the foundation for effective ministry in that congregation for years to come. Its aim is to help the new pastor to start well and to "hit the ground running." For the new pastor, I would advise that you begin at the beginning and read all the way through (actually, you need to read this book before you accept the call).

However, this book will also help both clergy and lay leaders currently serving in congregations. It will help you to understand some of the dynamics that occur in your church and give you fresh eyes through which to see your church. You will find a certain amount of theory that will help you understand your congregation. If you already understand the congregational dynamics of your church, you can use this book as a toolkit to fine-tune various areas of your church's life. So, if you are a clergy or lay leader and are not new to your congregation, you will want to read this book in the following order:

- Read the first three chapters in order to understand the dynamics of the interplay between congregational size, life cycle, and leadership.
- Read the first section of Chapter 5 about the Genesis story of a congregation.
- Read Chapter 6 on bringing about change.
- *Then*, go to the chapter that catches your interest.

C.S. Lewis once wrote that the way to absorb a book is to read it through first for the larger story; then re-read it in order to really enjoy it. Similarly, read each chapter through first. Then, go back and explore the sections that you'd like to focus on.

You'll find two different icons that indicate places for you to reflect. These are designed to help you reflect on what you're reading. Space has been left for you to write notes.

*You'll want to stop at the places in text where you see the light bulb, which are labeled **Quick Insight**. These brief exercises will give you an extra tidbit of information that will help you understand your congregation using the information at hand.*

*There are other places to stop that are designated by a magnifying glass. These are labeled **Closer Look**. These brief exercises are more process-oriented questions and will require a bit more time in reflection. These are not designed to provide quick answers but are rather more reflective questions.*

I'll close with a few comments about what I would call the philosophical underpinnings.

Congregational Development, Not Church Growth

This is a book about congregational development, not church growth. Weeds grow, but they are not necessarily healthy for the garden. The aim of this book is to help you as a leader in your church to develop a healthy, vital church.

Having said this, however, healthy things do grow. This is true of both plants and people. Given a proper amount of soil, nutrients, water, and light, plants will do what comes naturally; that is, they will grow. Sometimes, plants cease to grow because they are root bound (i.e., they grow as large as they can until their roots take up the whole flowerpot), and there is no more room for them to grow because the flowerpot is simply too small. When writing about the spiritual journey of individuals, medieval theologians would talk about obex. An obex is an obstacle, or a barricade. For a person to grow spiritually, it is necessary at times to remove the obex that is the obstacle to growth.

Often, our churches don't grow because there are unseen obstacles that have hindered the growth that is otherwise natural to the life of the church. If we, as leaders, can recognize those obstacles to growth and replace those obstacles with healthy practices, the church will grow naturally—with, of course, a life-giving gospel that is proclaimed, and with prayer, and with the work of the Holy Spirit.

So, this is not the final word on congregational development. Nor is it so theoretical that it will put you to sleep and make you think that congregational development is just for the experts. Hopefully, this book provides a balance between the theoretical and the practical: enough theory to give you the larger picture of what's really going on in your congregation, plenty of exercises to give you insight into your congregation, and lots of ideas that will improve any church.

Section 1

Understanding the Congregation

Chapter 1

Understanding Congregational Size Dynamics

For which of you, intending to build a tower,
does not first sit down and estimate the cost,
to see whether he has enough to complete it?

—Luke 14:28

Developing a congregation is simply the task of developing people; making disciples. However, there are really two levels of disciple-making: one is the micro level, the one-on-one process of helping a person grow in faith; the other is the macro level, that is, the process of mobilizing people. Most churches that get stuck often do so at the macro level. Clergy are trained in seminary to think theologically and to provide pastoral care to individuals; they are not trained, however, to mobilize people. They are trained to write theological papers and to conduct liturgy; they are not trained to develop ministries. This chapter provides a way of looking at the local congregation through the lens of congregational size dynamics to help leaders understand their church as a corporate entity. Groups of people when gathered together in various numbers relate to their leader and to each other in fairly predictable ways. Certain practices that make a group effective at one size will make it ineffective at a different size.

Although there are many factors that will affect a church's growth, one of the most common is the ability or lack of ability of the pastoral leader to adapt her style of leadership to the size of congregation that she is serving. Often, churches will find their growth limited because of invisible but very real size dynamics that keep the church at that certain size. The church has gotten used to being a certain size and will perpetuate the practices that make them effective at that size; they have grown comfortable with their ways of relating to one another as a congregation.

Although they may articulate a desire to grow, they often want to grow only while maintaining the current way of relating to the pastoral leader and to one another. Some churches will grow because they are able to adapt their system to mobilize the laity effectively. Other churches will plateau or decline in size to fit the comfort level of the system and leader that is in place.

This way of viewing the church as a system is theologically blind. These unseen limiters affect both "liberal" and "conservative" churches as well as "broad" churches. No church is immune. You may have the best theology in the world—from your perspective—but your church will be limited in its ability to grow because of its inability to change the way the leadership and congregation relate to each another.

Many times when church leaders first learn about congregational size dynamics, they get awfully excited. For example, they will write that their mission is to become a program-sized congregation. Attaining a larger church size does not constitute a valid mission. Lay people are not really motivated by growing their church larger. Mission is about reaching people with the good news of Jesus Christ; it is not about growing to a particular size. There is nothing intrinsically holy or salvific by being one size and not another. The real need is for churches to be good stewards of the gifts and resources that God has given them in fulfilling the Great Commission and the Great Commandments that Jesus gave his Church. Understanding congregational size dynamics is a tool for facilitating more effective ministry.

A Comment about Attendance versus Membership

Often when people talk about the size of their church they will say, "We have more than 400 members" or "250 families." That is a particularly unhelpful statement. In my experience, most of our church membership rolls are terribly out of date. I know of one church that had more than 150 members on their rolls for whom they had no current address.

The number of baptized members listed in a typical mainline denominational church bears no real relationship to the everyday dynamics of that congregation. Most churches will have many more members listed than those who are actively involved in the life of the congregation. A church that has 650 members with 150 average Sunday attendance is vastly different from a congregation with 500 members and 350 average Sunday attendance. The larger membership church with the smaller attendance will generally have fewer financial resources, fewer leaders, and fewer programs—and effectively fewer people to minister to—than the church with fewer members but more people actually attending. Scratch below the surface of the first church and you'll likely find many members who have moved away, died, or are no longer meaningfully connected to the church.

***Quick Insight**: Is your Sunday attendance-to-membership ratio 25 percent or less (i.e., Average Sunday Attendance divided by Baptized Membership; for example, 400 Baptized Members divided into 100 Average Sunday Attendance equals 25 percent)? If so, your church is in the "red zone," indicating that you've got your work cut out for you.*

We therefore concern ourselves with active participants rather than active or inactive members. Leaders may feel a need to be concerned about inactive members as a pastoral concern; however, the leaders who want to develop their congregation will be wise if they focus first on discipling and mobilizing the people who are actively attending before addressing their concerns about inactive people.

Realizing that the church has a large number of "phantom" members, the new pastor may be tempted to "clean the rolls" in order to begin her ministry with a clean slate. Don't do that.

There are several reasons not to clean the church's membership rolls in the first several years of a new pastor's tenure. First, a large reduction in membership at the beginning of a pastorate sends a wrong message to the congregation that the pastor is more concerned about the number of members than about the members as individuals. Also, an initial first-year reduction in membership silently communicates to the congregation that the church is in decline. A further problem is that the new pastor might drop people off the rolls that need to be visited, hence sending the message that she does not really care for those who may have been hurt in the past. It is better to ignore the membership numbers altogether than to fix it early in the pastor's tenure.

Sizing Up the Congregation

Why did our approach to congregational development change? Why did we begin to consider congregational size dynamics as a way of analyzing our churches? First, in the early 1980s, we began to notice that our denomination had been in serious membership decline for more than 15 years since its high membership mark in 1965. Second, more than two thirds of our churches at that time were either plateauing or declining. Third, clergy trained in the fast-growth 1950s were serving in the no-growth 1980s. They were not prepared for pastoring in this changed context. Fourth, we drastically reduced the number of new churches we were planting as a denomination and settled into a consolidation mode. Finally, we found that we were growing older as a denomination and not drawing younger families and individuals. So, a few forward-thinking people began to ask what was really going on inside our churches. Arlin Rothauge, former Congregational Development Officer for the Episcopal Church, and then Kevin Martin, then Canon for Congregational Development in the Diocese of Texas, helped Episcopal churches—as well as many other denominational churches—understand that this decline could actually be stemmed and that we could help lead our churches to greater health and growth through an understanding of congregational dynamics.

In 1982, Arlin Rothauge published a little booklet, *Sizing Up the Congregation,* which opened up a whole new way of understanding congregations from the perspective of size dynamics.[1] This booklet categorized churches according to numbers of active members and showed the dynamics of the relationships between the leader and the congregation. He suggested four sizes, as shown in the table below:

Name	Active members
Family	0–50
Pastoral	50–150
Program	150–350
Corporation	350+

Rothauge's analysis helped congregational leaders understand the interplay between leaders and followers and evangelism.

In 1995, Kevin Martin did a little fine tuning of Rothauge's analysis. First, he changed the basic subject group from active members to average Sunday attendance. Determining active members was difficult and led to analyses that simply did not fit Rothauge's otherwise insightful paradigm. Second, he changed the numerical categories based on his observations of churches that he had worked with in the Diocese of Texas. Third, and most significantly, he observed that many churches had a difficult time moving from the pastoral to program size. In response, he posited a fifth size category: the transitional-sized church. Finally, he changed the designation of corporate-sized church to resource-sized. Designating a church as corporate, he reasoned, seemed a bit sterile and, well, corporate-sounding rather than pastoral, and the significant aspect of this larger sized church is that it has an abundance of resources. Martin's size categories are as follows:

Name	Average Sunday attendance
Family	5–75
Pastoral	76–140
Transitional	141–225
Program	226–400
Resource	401+

So, let's look at these size dynamics a bit more closely using Kevin Martin's analysis.

The Family-Sized Church

The family-sized church has an average Sunday attendance of up to 75. These churches are typically located in smaller towns. They function much as a family does and are often made up of a couple of interrelated families in the leadership of the church. Not everyone in the church is a member of the extended family, but one prominent extended family is often at the center of influence.

Closer Look: *If your church resembles this size, notice whom people look at when they talk or whom people seem to discuss things with before a decision is made? You'll probably find the matriarch or patriarch in this group.*

The ordained person in this size of church is not the head of the congregation (family). Instead, the ordained person functions as the chaplain to the congregation. The congregation expects only pastoral care from the pastor—counseling, prayers at appropriate occasions, hospital visits, weddings, funerals, and so on—but the real decisions affecting the church are made by long-standing members of the congregation. The true leader in this congregational family system is designated as the matriarch or patriarch. This person is usually a long-term member of both the congregation and the community and will typically have children and grandchildren in the congregation. The church is really a set of a few extended family units with a few other friends as well.

Although the vestry is the stated lay leadership circle, usually the vestry will defer to the matriarch/patriarch. It is not unusual to have a vestry make a decision only to have the same vestry reverse itself a month later after everyone has talked to the matriarch/patriarch of the congregation. Woe be to the pastor who serves a family-sized church who really believes that she is the leader of the congregation.

The strength of this congregation is in its stability. The weakness is its low expectations. Success for this church is in keeping the doors open.

The Pastoral-Sized Church

The pastoral-sized church has an average Sunday attendance of 76 to 140. The first major shift occurs in terms of leadership. This church is clergy-centered. The role of the ordained person can be described as the *pater familias*. That is, instead of functioning primarily as the chaplain in the congregation, this ordained person is the focal point of all activities.

The pastor is, indeed, the leader of the congregation (however, be sure to read Chapter 3 on leadership levels and Chapter 6 on managing change before feeling too overconfident about what it means to be the leader of the congregation). The pastor in this size of church is usually expected to give her opinion on flower arrangements and paint colors, to assign the setting up of chairs, pray before parish gatherings, be the first to the hospital, and so on. The pastoral-sized church pastor is the primary evangelist in the congregation as well. She will be the primary drawing card to bring new people into the congregation.

This is the "friends" church, where everybody among the group of friends knows everyone else. Lives are intertwined. People are attracted to this church because of the intimacy among the congregation. A person can miss church one Sunday, return the next, and five different people will ask what they have been doing or how their trip was. A church of this size can give to its members a real sense of belonging and family.

Quick Insight: *Read over your parish profile or listen to what parishioners say about their church. If they describe themselves as a "warm and friendly church," they are likely to be a pastoral-sized church.*

The role of the vestry at this level is to serve as the unpaid staff of the church. Because a church at this size generally has only one full-time staff member, namely, the pastor, the vestry members are often the ones who carry out the plans of the rector and the congregation. When the vestry of the pastoral-sized church sees itself as simply decision makers for the congregation, the pastor becomes overworked, and the church is not set up for the appropriate and healthy transition to the larger size.

The strength of this congregation is in its stability. Assuming that the physical property of the church is in good repair, this church can sustain itself for a long time. It is tremendously enjoyable and fulfilling to be in a pastoral-sized church—as long as your expectations are not too high.

Worship services are provided on a regular basis, and the congregants generally know what to expect in them. Individuals can rise in leadership and responsibility. Each member expects, and can usually get, equal access to the pastor. She is always available for counseling as well as for more personal social occasions.

The weakness of this congregation is in its predictability. The programs offered by this congregation are generic and small. Don't expect a very large choir or for the choir to sing very challenging music. The youth group is often no larger than a Bible study. Planning for this church is usually based on "what did we do last year?" This year's budget looks suspiciously like last year's, and like the year before that, and the year before that one. . . . Often leaders are tired, because there are more leadership positions than there are emerging leaders, so people are often weary from having too many church responsibilities.

Further, the pastor has the primary responsibility of incorporating newcomers into the ongoing life of the church. The key to making newcomers feel like they belong is for them to have a relationship with the pastor. In this size of church, the pastor is the glue that holds all these relationships together—both newcomers as well as long-time members.

The Program-Sized Church

We now jump ahead in the order of Martin's categories to look at the program-sized church, because we have to understand the program-sized church before we can understand the intermediate transitional-sized church.

The program-sized church has an average Sunday attendance of 226 to 400. Whereas the spiritual nourishment in a pastoral-sized church occurs primarily through a relationship with the pastor, in the program-sized church most spiritual nourishment takes place though the programs of the church—and supplemented by the pastor. This church is noted by the presence of activity and program offerings. There is a place to land for just about everyone in this size of church.

The typical parishioner in a program-sized church knows the same number of people as the typical parishioner in a pastoral-sized church; however, there are simply more people for the parishioner in the program-sized church not to know. The quality of relationships is no less significant or meaningful, although it may seem so to the average pastoral-sized church member. One often hears people in a pastoral-sized church say, "Now, we don't want to become one of those megachurches."

The role of the pastor changes from the *pater familias* in the pastoral-sized church to the chief administrator in the program-sized church. The pastor is still at the center of the life of the congregation, but her role has shifted. Newcomers in a program-sized church don't expect to know the senior pastor on a personal basis. They may be in church five times before exchanging more than 25 words with the pastor. Likewise, parishioners don't usually expect a hospital visit from the senior pastor; although it *is* expected in a time of crisis or real need. The senior pastor spends her time planning with other staff members and lay leaders in the congregation, recruiting new leaders, facilitating the activities in the congregation, and keeping the programs running smoothly.

The clergy person who derives her primary satisfaction in parish ministry through performing direct, hands-on pastoral care will be very dissatisfied in a church of this size. Most pastoral ministry is lay-led, because the ordained person spends so much of her time mobilizing lay leaders. She must have most of her ministry needs satisfied through her work with her staff and other leaders. If she spends too much time in pastoral care, her leaders will go uncared for and will not be properly supervised and developed.

This is an example of the Pareto principle, named for the Italian economist Vilfredo Pareto. He developed a mathematical formula to describe the unequal distribution of wealth in Italy where, he determined, 80 percent of the wealth of the country was owned by 20 percent of the people. The value of the Pareto principle is in helping the leader to focus on the 20 percent that will produce the greatest results. Because the program-sized church is most effective through its programs, the pastor who spends too much time with individual pastoral care is actually misserving her leaders. Although she may get lots of strokes for her pastoral care by individuals, her leaders may go floundering, and the net result is that a few people are very happy with her, but the church declines as it becomes mismanaged and its leaders inadequately supervised.

Quick Insight: *As the rector of a program-sized congregation, look over your calendar for a typical week. How much of your time is spent with leaders responsible for others in ministry?*

The vestry of a church of this size serves as the vision-casting, communicating, and policy-forming leadership group of the church. With the senior pastor, they grasp the vision of the church and keep it on course in fulfilling the vision. The day-to-day operations of the church are directed by the staff.

It is a real challenge for a person who has served on the vestry of a smaller church to adjust to leadership of a larger church such as this. They tend to look at the church through smaller eyes and want to be involved in the day-to-day management operations of the church as was their practice in the smaller church.

The strength of this church is in its program offerings. Senior pastors can come and go; as long as they don't do significant damage to the congregation, the programs will carry this congregation along. Most of the staff are trained and paid and generally carry out their responsibilities quite well. People, particularly in suburban areas, are attracted to program-sized churches because they have a program that will meet most generic needs and interests for youth, children, men, women, and so on.

Incorporation of newcomers is accomplished through this church's programs. The assimilation process is based on a programmatic offering. Classes and get-togethers are offered on a regular basis—as compared to the pastoral-sized church's approach to newcomers' classes: "whenever we have enough newcomers to need a class." A church of this size has many side doors into the congregation, such as Mothers Day Out, the choir, Bible studies, youth ministries, and so on.

The Transitional-Sized Church

Now we return to discuss the transitional-sized church, generally having an average Sunday attendance of 141 to 225. (However, be careful not to view these attendance categories as a "hard and fast rule." Some transitional-sized and even program-sized churches are actually overgrown pastoral-sized churches with overperforming clergy.) Designating a church as "transitional-sized" is another way of saying that it is a sort of hybrid church—it is not pastoral-sized, and it is not program-sized. Churches of the other sizes usually function in a state of equilibrium. There is never a state of equilibrium in the transitional-sized church.

Kevin Martin says that the transitional-sized church is 75 percent pastoral and 75 percent program. What he means is that at any given time, 75 percent of the congregation is expecting the church to function as a pastoral-sized church, and 75 percent of the congregation is expecting the church to function as a program-sized church—all at the same time! (Yes, 75 plus 75 does not add up to 100!) That is the challenge of the transitional-sized church. In fact, some of those individuals have their own contradictory expectations for the church, wanting it to be both small and intimate while at the same time offering the quality programs characteristic of a larger church.

The role of the pastor is threefold: non-anxious presence, vision caster, and developer of leaders. Because of these competing and contradictory expectations, this is the most stressed congregation and the most stressed pastor. Thus, the effective pastor will be a non-anxious presence, because almost everyone else is anxious. The congregation has both rising expectations for future growth as well as fear of the loss of intimacy from no longer being a smaller congregation.

One of the ways of being a non-anxious presence is for the pastor to be an effective vision caster. What the wise pastor knows is that as the church grows a little larger, there is light at the end of the tunnel—and it is not an oncoming train. Experience with other congregations growing from transitional- to program-sized churches shows that something amazing happens when the church grows upward to an average Sunday attendance of 225 to 250. As it moves out of transitional size and into the program size, things begin to "settle down" emotionally for the congregation. An almost palpable feeling of calm begins to pervade the congregation. At this larger size, although the congregation is just as busy as it was at the smaller size, the healthy stability of predictability and confidence begins to pervade the congregation. Vision will empower people to stretch and sacrifice through the anxiety-laden transitional size to that 225 to 250 period of increased stability. If the pastor does not make this transition herself in her vision casting among the congregation, she will "grow the church down" to her own comfort level.

The third role of the pastor is to be a developer of leaders. She must develop leaders because a church of this size is characterized by a number of programs that "haven't yet arrived." The transitional-sized church has lots of needs and interests but not always that "critical mass" necessary to have a fully functioning ministry in individual areas. It never has enough leaders. In fact, the best description for this size of church is the Madeleine Kahn character Lili Von Schtupp in the movie *Blazing Saddles,* who sings, "I'm tired." So many lay leaders are tired in the transitional-sized church because there are not enough leaders to fill all the roles for the jobs that need to be done. It is crucial for the growth of the church that the pastor transition from being the primary provider of ministry to being the developer of leaders.

The vestry is also transitioning, from the unpaid staff of the church to the vision-casting, policy-enabling board that fosters the growth that is both natural and unnatural to this church. It is in this size of church that the two church sizes compete for supremacy. In the smaller church with an average Sunday attendance of 3 to 225, there is internal pressure to preserve intimacy. As the church begins to grow, somewhere around an average Sunday attendance of 120 to 250 there is an external pressure to provide quality programming. If the vestry does not transition to accommodate this more complex entity, the internal pressure to preserve intimacy will overpower the external pressure to provide quality programming.

The transitional-sized church is like an adolescent boy going through a growth spurt. His voice is changing; his clothes don't fit; he feels awkward and gangly. Just as it takes patience to help the adolescent through this challenging time in his life, it also takes patience to help the transitional-sized church through this awkward time in its life. The difference is that the adolescent *will* become a teenager; without proper guidance and appropriate changes at various levels, the transitional-sized church will *not* make it through to a program size.

There are many, many churches that had the potential for growth cut short because either the pastor or the lay governing board failed to make the transition to a more complex way of being the church.

Closer Look: *You've identified your church as a transitional-sized church. Take a mental survey of your congregation. Which do you need right away: more leaders? more space? more financial resources? more time? or all of these all at the same time?*

The Resource-Sized Church

We turn now to the largest size under consideration: the resource-sized church, with an average Sunday attendance of 401+. The hallmark of this size of church is excellence. The facilities are top-notch, the music is well done; the nursery is clean and neat and staffed by well-trained personnel; the printed materials are all attractive.

This church has a large, professional staff. There is much room for advancement of lay leaders. The resource-sized church will often hire lay leaders from within the congregation to new staff positions. They are the ones who are most conversant with and supportive of the vision of this congregation. Further, this church is noted for its specialized programs offered to smaller and more discrete subgroups within the culture.

This church is usually not one congregation but rather is often made up of smaller congregations within the larger church. It may have a small-group structure or some other way to break down the congregation into more identifiable and socially cohesive subgroups. Parishioners will give up a close relationship with the senior pastor in favor of the quality programs and ministries offered by the resource-sized church.

The senior pastor is more like the president of a university, managing several deans as well as a large staff of a very complex and diverse congregation. She must be able to articulate the unique vision of this church and keep a large staff on-task and living the vision of the congregation. The effective senior pastor, then, is a motivator and is more of a symbol of unity, stability, and energy for the congregation.

The vestry functions in a fashion similar to that of the program-sized church, affirming the vision of the church and giving permission for new nongeneric ministries to be started. (*Nongeneric* ministries are those ministries beyond the basics of Sunday school, choir, altar guild, and so on, found in the vast majority of transitional and smaller sized churches.) In a resource-sized church, the vestry must focus its resources on the ever-expanding mission of the church. If the mission doesn't expand, the church will begin to plateau, and decline will soon follow. Because of its size and the general stability of its financial base, decline in this church is often imperceptible by the vast majority of its parishioners.

Likewise, newcomers are drawn to the church because of the program offerings of this larger church. The nongeneric ministries of resource-sized churches bring in new people that smaller churches will not attract. Often these larger churches provide a safety valve or way station for exiles from smaller congregations in conflict or will attract people from smaller congregations that do not provide the quality programs, such as youth ministry, youth program, and so on, that they are looking for.

Closer Look: *Be careful to base the analysis of your congregation on the characteristics of your congregation and not simply on the average Sunday attendance numbers. Just as some transitional-sized churches are simply overgrown pastoral-sized churches, some churches with an average Sunday attendance of between 400 and 500 are simply overgrown program-sized churches.*

Growth Keys in the Various Congregational Sizes

A shorthand way of understanding the difference between smaller churches and larger churches, according to Canon Keith Brown, former Missioner for Congregational Development in the Diocese of San Joaquin, is that for smaller churches, the purpose for existing is "to be." The overall purpose for larger churches is "to do." Smaller churches can't compete with the program offerings of larger churches. They make up for this with their close-knit nature of relationships. Certain people are attracted to smaller churches precisely because they are small.

Smaller churches offer close, personal relationships. When I miss church, people notice. When I am sick, people call or come by. For a church to exist, "to be," so that those life-giving relationships can occur in the context of a worshiping community, is a good thing and something to be nurtured.

Larger churches offer programs that also meet the more programmatic needs of its members, whether they are age-graded Sunday school, music of a certain quality, small-group gatherings with people of similar age and interests, missions involvement, and so on. These churches exist "to do," and people are attracted to churches that "do" things that will meet their felt needs.

Smaller churches that have been in existence for more than 20 years generally don't have much prospect for numerical growth. In fact, to talk about church growth only emphasizes to them how small they are. The thinking goes like this: "We can't offer the programs of those larger churches, so how can we grow?"

Growth in Family-Sized Congregations

For many family-sized churches, success amounts to keeping the doors open year after year. Because they cannot compete with the program offerings of larger churches, these churches should concern themselves with health rather than growth. Leaders should ask, "What will make us a healthier church?" So, rather than talking about church growth in the smaller churches, it is better to talk about church health. Most churches that aim for growth generally miss it. Most churches that aim for health generally find that growth will naturally follow where there is health. Thus, the family-sized church will want to focus on healthy relationships among its members and relationally based pastoral care.

Healthy churches reach out beyond themselves. In terms of outreach and missions, these churches should find one identifiable ministry that the majority of church members can support and participate in. Remember the saying by Mother Teresa, "Do small things in big ways." For example, the church could actively support (with both people and financial resources) a local food bank, a prison ministry in the area (such as Kairos), or an annual short-term mission trip to a foreign country. To try to do all three will stretch the lean people-resources of this church. The family-sized church might also partner with a resource-sized church in a nearby city to be a part of their team.

How does the pastoral leader effect change in this type of congregation? Generally, effecting change in a family-sized congregation is not desired among members of the congregation. However, the ongoing management of the affairs of the church is best accomplished by working closely with, and enlisting the support of, the matriarch/patriarch. In one church that I served, I played golf on a weekly basis with the patriarch of the congregation (a godly and beloved man). Although he did not serve on the vestry, I ran everything I was thinking by him. He would make suggestions and was a tremendous support. My effectiveness in that congregation was based, not on my position as pastor, but on the respect and influence of this beloved and godly man in this congregation and his wise and generous counsel to me.

Incorporation of newcomers is usually done through the matriarch/patriarch. Let the newcomer get to know this person. The pastor can introduce this newcomer to people in the church, but the matriarch/patriarch will open the door to the newcomer in the life of the congregation.

Some people will ask, "What if we don't have a matriarch or patriarch? How do we get one?" You don't. Matriarchs and patriarchs in congregations simply emerge. They are a natural by-product of the church system and history in that local place. The ordained person will need to know who the influencers are in the congregation and work through the issues of governance with them.

Growth in Pastoral-Sized Congregations

As is true for the family-sized church, congregational health is also job number one for the pastoral-sized church. Although the quest for pastoral care should not absorb all the attention of the church, pastoral care is crucial for a pastoral-sized church. People in these smaller churches expect to be noticed and cared for (and rightly so). Good pastoral care is like getting to first base for this church. You can't get to second base without first accomplishing decent pastoral care.

In terms of governance, many of the leaders of pastoral-sized churches feel overworked—and underappreciated. They feel overworked because pastoral-sized churches often structure themselves similar to the larger churches that they know, with a multiplicity of committees and programs that are inappropriate for a church of their size. A church of this size will have fifteen to twenty-eight leaders. You don't want to keep your best leaders occupied with committee meetings when the church doesn't have enough Sunday school teachers. It may be necessary to "right-size" (that is, downsize) the church to match the most crucial ministries with the number of leaders that the church has.

The leaders will want to ask the question, "What are our core goods and services?" Make sure that these are adequately covered. Remember, the primary issue is congregational health rather than congregational growth.

The pastor is crucial in terms of incorporation. The hallmark of the pastoral-sized church is the central nature of the pastor. Therefore, it is important for the pastor to connect with every newcomer, inviting them into her home for social occasions. The pastor should join a local service organization (Lions' Club, Kiwanis, etc.), must be involved in public affairs (attend the Friday night football games or Thursday night basketball games, and so on), and have a good relationship with the local ministerial association.

As the church begins to approach an average Sunday attendance of 110, the pastor will begin to approach the upward limit of pastoral relationships that she can healthily manage. If the church is to continue the growth that has occurred, the pastor must begin having lay people bear some of the pastoral care responsibilities.

This is what typically happens when a pastor reaches the upper limit of her ability to sustain the number of pastoral relationships by herself in her cure. In a pastoral-sized church, the pastor appropriately functions as the chief evangelist and assimilator of four to five new families. She spends extra time with them, getting to know them, and welcoming them into the church family. They like this new pastor and feel very much cared for in their new church. However, because the pastor has spent extra time with these new families, incorporating them into the life of the congregation, then four or five families who have been a part of the congregation now feel ignored by their pastor. They begin to resent the newer families. Rumors begin: "Our pastor doesn't really care about us anymore. All she cares about are the new people in the church. The church is getting too big. She's concerned about numbers now and not people." Soon, although the church has grown with four to five new families, it also loses four to five new families who find a variety of reasons to leave the church.

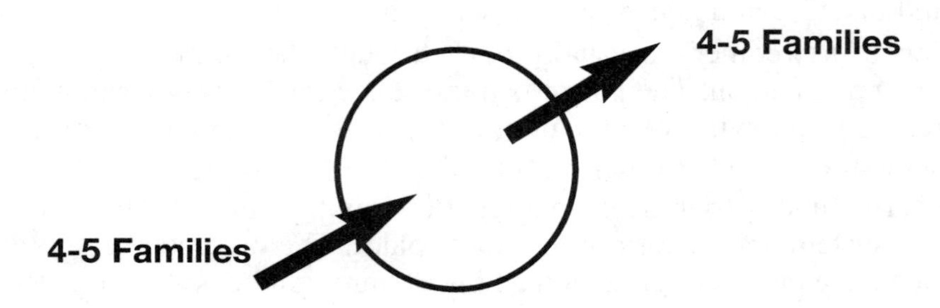

After a while, unless the pastor learns new management skills, the church as a system learns that it cannot absorb any new people. Even when new families and individuals join the church, they will be accompanied by an attendant loss of an equal number of people. Thus, the system becomes homeostatic at the upper end level of the number of pastoral relationships that the pastor can sustain by herself and then will stop growing.

Quick Insight: *The skills that foster growth in a pastoral-sized church and make it healthy may be an obstacle to growth as the church moves into the transitional and program sizes.*

How can the church grow beyond the pastoral-sized level? This brings us to the transitional-sized church.

Growth in Transitional-Sized Congregations

For a church to grow beyond a pastoral-sized church, the pastor must learn to deal with complexity. She can no longer have her primary identity as the one who ministers to everyone in her church and must instead multiply herself and work through others. She must shift from being a provider of ministry to a developer of leaders. Her mode of pastoring (managing) needs to develop from a shepherd mode of pastoring to a rancher mode of pastoring. Simply put: a pastor knows each of the sheep by name; a rancher knows each of the ranch hands by name.

In *Making the Small Church Effective,*[2] Carl Dudley describes the small church pastor as a "lover" of members of the congregation. Each knows that they are individually loved and cared for by the pastor. However, for the church to grow in numbers, it must grow in complexity, and the pastor must give up some of the intimacy with everyone individually in the congregation.

The pastor must learn to be a rancher, to manage and delegate responsibilities for ministry and caregiving to other lay leaders. Where does the pastor get these qualified lay leaders? She has to develop them. She is still responsible for the pastoral care for the whole congregation, but she doesn't do all the ministry herself.

It is awfully tempting for a growing church to begin all sorts of ministries at this size. The transitional-sized church must resist the temptation to do too much. It has more and more people requesting more and more programs, but it doesn't have enough leaders to go around; nor does it always have a critical mass of participants in certain programs. So, this size of church has to pick and choose what it can do well. It is starting to learn that "good enough, isn't," and that more and more people are expecting things to be done with excellence.

The leaders of the church must learn to do fewer things with excellence rather than many things with mediocrity. They must exercise the discipline never to allow a program or ministry to begin without a leader in place. They must understand that if God calls a church to provide a given ministry, he will supply the leader. If there is no leader, one must assume that either God has not called the church to do that ministry or the leader hasn't emerged, yet; but, in any event, God wants a leader to be in place before the ministry is launched. It may be a good ministry, but without a leader, the timing is never right to launch a new ministry or program.

One area the transitional-sized church must grow is the area of missions and outreach. At this larger size, the church must expand its missions and outreach involvement rather than simply maintaining what has previously been done in this area. Expansion of mission and outreach is appropriate to the stewardship gifts and responsibilities of a growing congregation. People are not drawn to an ingrown, self-absorbed congregation. Rather, the congregation must now embrace its outward-growing focus.

Incorporation of newcomers becomes increasingly more programmatic. Rather than holding a newcomer's class whenever there are enough newcomers in the church, the growing church will hold regular classes for newcomers. This class will present ways to get involved in the life of the congregation, the history of the congregation, the vision and values of the congregation, and what are the stewardship expectations of members.

Growth in Program-Sized Congregations

This church is noted for all its basic programs that are well executed; it has a growing and more professional staff; its facilities are well cared for; and its financial condition is fairly stable. The challenge for the program-sized congregation is to avoid complacency. How does the program-sized church grow?

This church grows through its programs that provide a variety of side entrance doors into the church. Thus, it is of crucial importance for the senior pastor to develop an effective staff. The changes that must occur have several implications for the church staff and leaders.

First, the staff must grow in their skills and knowledge of their particular areas of responsibility. Their overarching responsibility is not simply to maintain or oversee their programs but to develop them. They are called to expand their ministries year after year. Continuing education, skill development, and quality improvement are crucial for the staff.

Second, when it comes to adding new staff, the church must staff for tomorrow's needs rather than yesterday's. For example, if faced with the decision of whether to hire a clergy person to provide pastoral care for the older members of the congregation or to hire a full-time youth pastor, the growing church will hire for the future need rather than yesterday's need. Also, it is tempting for a church of this size to want to add an ordained person to the staff for its next staff position. It is more strategically advisable to hire a qualified lay person to reach a new target population or to complement the skills of the rector than to hire a clergy person to do more pastoral care.

Third, the congregational leaders will want to review each of the basic programs of the church and make sure that each is done with excellence. There are no cutting corners at the level of a congregation's "basic goods and services." The church cannot expand its ministry reach until it covers all its foundational programs. If there is a gap, people will notice it and rightly perceive that the church is out of balance.

Finally, the program-sized congregation must focus on developing leaders at every level of the church's life. Churches at this level will generally attract visitors because of their sheer size. People visit these churches because they expect them to provide programs that will meet their needs. If leaders are not developed and nourished, the ever-expanding programs will fall into disarray, and the commitment to excellence necessary for a church of this size will go unmet.

Growth in Resource-Sized Congregations

One of the positive aspects of both program- and resource-sized churches is their financial stability. The challenge for those churches is not to be satisfied with the status quo. The temptation, especially for the resource-sized church, is "if we keep doing things the way we've been doing, we'll be just fine." Maintaining the size of the congregation is not too difficult. The staff is very professional; they are used to working hard; and these churches offer excellent programs. Our understanding of congregational life cycles in Chapter 2 will show why churches must continually be improving and looking for the next growth phase. Without a growing edge of ministry and mission, the stability that is positive in the life of a resource-sized congregation will eventually turn into decline.

Vision is crucial for the resource-sized congregation. What makes this church unique? Why should people want to be a part of this congregation? The senior pastor of the resource-sized congregation is the chief motivator and communicator of what the church is uniquely about. With her preaching and teaching, the senior pastor establishes the priorities of the church that are in keeping with the vision of the congregation. For this size of church to remain effective, the vision of the church, through the senior pastor, keeps all the diverse and disparate ministries and staff all headed in the same direction.

Chapter 2
Understanding Church Growth Factors

To every thing there is a season,
and a time to every purpose under the heaven.

—Ecclesiastes 3:1

Churches are not static entities. They are living organisms. Not only is it important for the leader to understand the peculiar dynamics relative to the congregation's size, it is also important to understand where the congregation is in terms of its life cycle. It is not simply a matter of knowing how old the congregation is in terms of years. To be able to lead the congregation, the leader must understand where this congregation—as a living organism—is in the larger perspective of its ongoing life.

Congregational Life Cycle

All living things have life cycles, whether they are plants, trees, animals, empires, or humans. Many people have been a part of a small group, a Bible study group, a book discussion circle, or a bowling team and recognize this reality as well. The group makes plans to come together for a common purpose. They share the excitement of what the group will look like and become. One day, the group is born. Soon, new members join. After a while, the group is functioning well. The members know each other and can depend on each other. Then one day, one or two group members seem to miss a meeting or two. People find reasons to be absent. Finally, too many people miss gatherings too often, and the group either intentionally disbands or simply quits meeting. Sound familiar? It should. This is normal. This is the normal life cycle of a group.

Churches also have life cycles that follow this similar pattern. Ecclesiastes tells us that there is a time to be born and a time to die. In between those two periods, there is usually a time for growing or developing, a time of stability, and a time of declining. This is the typical life cycle and can be graphed as follows:

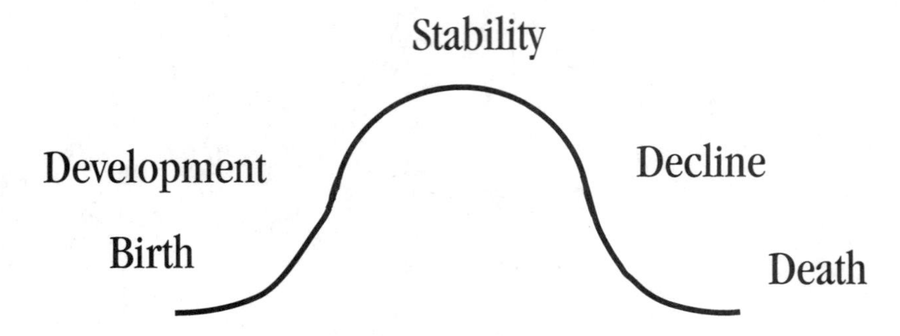

Here is a brief description of these phases:

- **Birth:** A new congregation emerges from the vision of certain persons. Birth is the culmination of the planning and dreaming stages. Resources are brought together, and the new entity emerges.
- **Development:** As the church grows, new people come. The sense of the congregation is that their best years are still to come. New ideas, new programs, an air of expectancy at what new things will emerge are all in the air of the congregation at this stage.
- **Stability:** Things are running smoothly at this stage. The congregation knows what to expect. Minor corrections are in order, but the sense of the congregation is, "If we just keep doing what we've been doing, we'll be all right."
- **Decline:** One day, people start to look around and begin to notice that the church has gotten a little "long in the tooth." They begin to notice that the neighborhood surrounding them has changed, deferred maintenance begins to be an issue, people may reminisce about and want to recapture "the way things used to be."
- **Death:** Decline reaches the point where the congregation begins to focus on surviving, marshaling its resources for its own preservation. It has lost its sense of mission and would be happy just to maintain where it had been. Its best years are truly behind them.

***Quick Insight**: Do your leaders talk about the future opportunities of the church or repairing the buildings and grounds? When did you last hire a new staff member to meet a growth need?*

The S-Curve

We have said that just as the natural course for humans is to be born, grow, stabilize, decline, and die, so it is natural for churches to do the same. However, before the eventuality of death sets in, churches can renew or prolong their life by giving birth before the active dying phase sets in. It looks graphically like this.

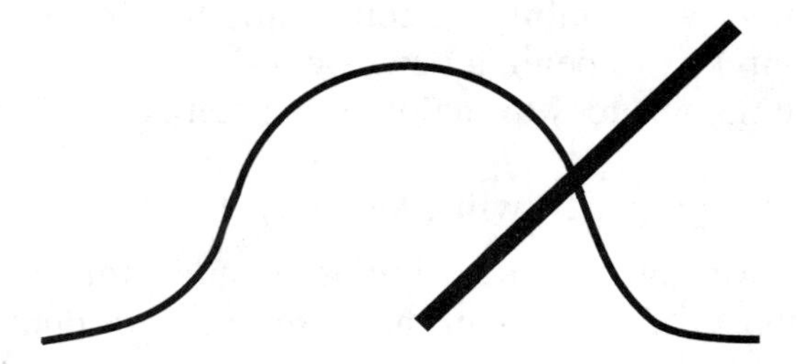

What results is what many would call an "S-curve."

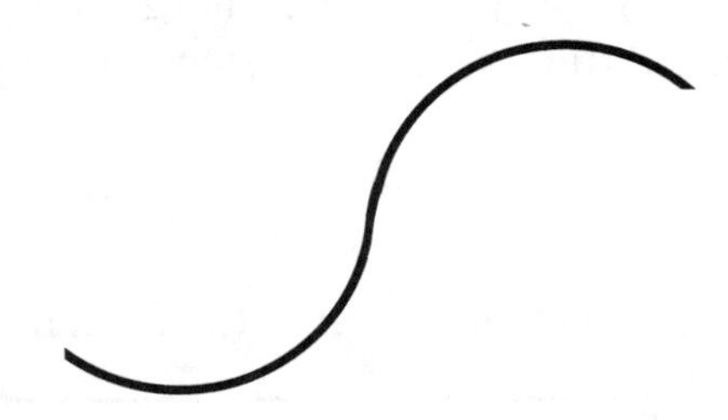

Scientists and mathematicians use the S-curve to represent the trends that occur in the life cycles of businesses, people, organizations, and many living things. A typical S-curve has an exponential portion in which the slope, representing growth, increases. At some point, the slope begins to decrease (there is always a downturn), and the curve then begins to round off. Unless there is an intervention, the natural course of life is to reach a peak, decline, and eventually to die.

The only way to prolong the life of the organization—in this discussion, a church—is to start a new S-curve. Thus, the organization must continually reinvent itself in order to avoid the decline and death that are natural to the uninterrupted life cycle.

The challenge is this: when to start the new S-curve, to catch the next wave. When things are going well, there seems to be no reason to change; life is stable. The attitude is prevalent: "so, don't rock the boat; things are going just fine" or "if it ain't broke, don't fix it." However, this is the paradox of success: start the new S-curve at the very point that things are still on their way up. The reason for this is found in the Second Law of Thermodynamics.

The Second Law of Thermodynamics

You may recall from high school or college physics the notion that the physical world is winding down. The Second Law of Thermodynamics, commonly known as the law of increased entropy, states that in a closed system, the quantity of energy remains the same while the quality of matter and energy deteriorates gradually over time. Entropy tells us that matter and energy in a system always deteriorate.

What the Second Law of Thermodynamics means for the church and the normal life cycle is that unless we pour new energy into the (church's) system, eventually the (church) system will deteriorate gradually over time. Let's summarize:

To overcome entropy, you must pour energy into the system

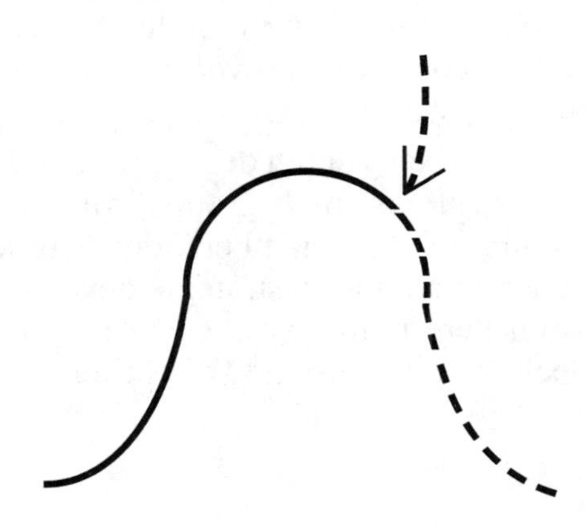

- The norm for a church's life cycle is birth, growth, stability, decline, and then death.
- The only way to prolong the life of the church is to begin a new S-curve.
- It takes more energy to add a new S-curve than it does to maintain the status quo of the congregation.
- To maintain the status quo means that the congregation will eventually decline and die.

(Now, be careful about initiating change. We don't want to initiate change for the sake of change. In Chapter 6, we'll explore what changes the leader can make and how to identify what changes need to be made in the congregation.)

If we return to our graphical illustration of the life cycle and the S-curve, we'll understand the need to pour energy into the system to keep entropy from setting in. Pouring new energy into the system should be for the purpose of starting a new S-curve, not simply to work harder in maintaining what had been once been successful. Generally, if we pour more energy into a declining church without being strategic in where we are pouring it, the result is "hastened decline" and not the prolongation of the life of the congregation.

The Paradox of Change

Now comes the question, "When is the best time to pour new energy into the system?"

The best time to begin a new S-curve is just before the period of stability sets in (point A in the graph). There are several reasons for this. It takes a certain amount of time and resources for the new change to set in. The second curve has to start before the first sets in. The second reason to start the S-curve before stability sets in is because the later you start the new S-curve, the more energy it takes to overcome the forces of entropy. It seems that it would be easier to initiate change when the curve starts to go downhill (point B in the graph), but that is when it takes even more energy. Attendance is down. People are discouraged. Morale is low. Resources are scarcer.

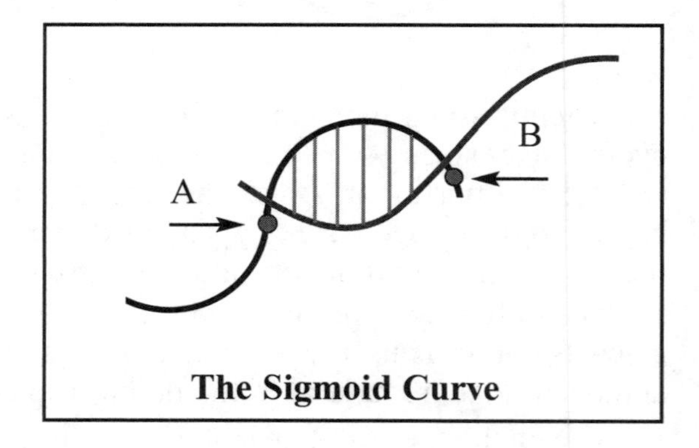

The Sigmoid Curve

This is what Charles Handy, British economist and author, calls the "paradox of change."[3] The time to start a new growth curve is when things are going well. The challenge for the organization is to begin building a new future, that is, to develop a new growth stream, while maintaining the current stream. He says that the people who lead the second curve are often not the people who led (and who maintain) the second curve. The responsibility of the leaders is to maintain the first curve long enough to support the early stages of the second curve.

One of the best examples of a church that has harnessed the power of the S-curve principle to realize continued growth is Christ Church, Episcopal, in Plano, Texas. Here is an illustration of their growth curves.

A more in-depth description of the story of Christ Church would include changes in such areas as the role of small groups, role of music and music leadership, adding and releasing and reassigning of staff members, development of new programs, approach to outreach, the role of adult education, and the strategic development of part-time and full-time staff, just to name a few. The point here is that you can't "rest in the nest." Complacency and comfortableness are signs that decline is just around the corner.

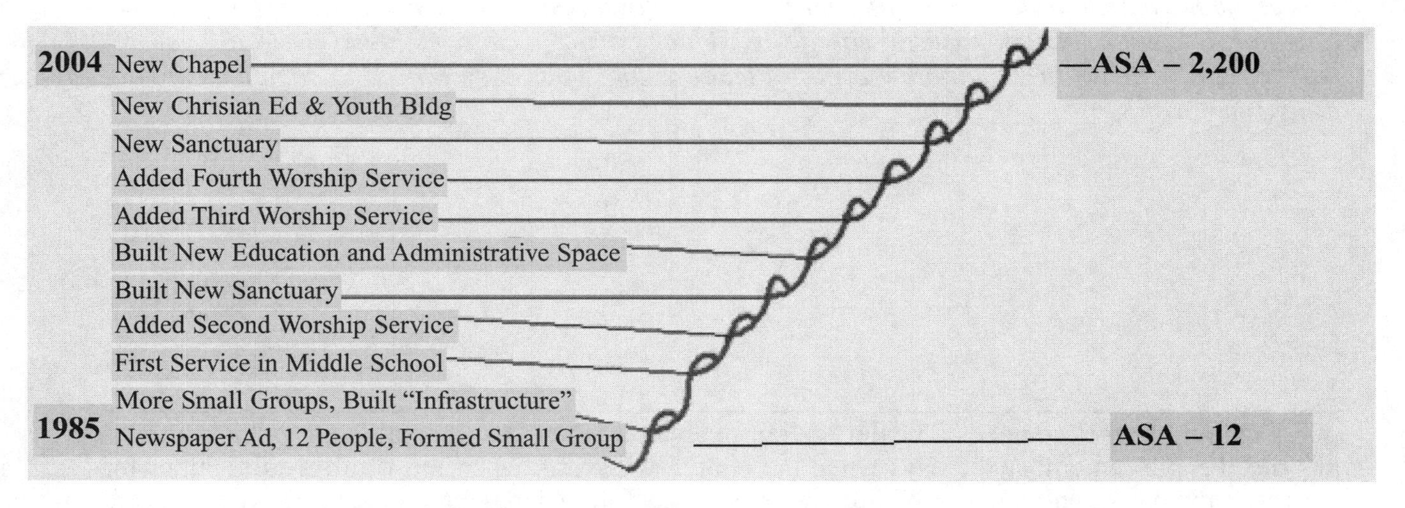

Leadership Needs at the Various Life-Cycle Phases

Because of the different phases in congregational life, it follows that churches need leaders with different skills, depending on which phase the church finds itself in.

During the *birth* phase, the church needs a leader who is both a vision caster and a catalyst. First, the leader must be able to cast a vision of a more desirable future that people will want to commit to, sacrifice for, and get passionate about. In addition, the emerging church needs leaders who are catalysts to get things done. Many grand visions are never realized because there were no leaders who could turn the vision into reality.

A church in the *formation* phase needs an organizer. Planning, coordinating, and implementation are all needed at this stage. The leaders here need to be able to discover and develop resources, as well as lead others to bring the hopes and dreams from the birth phase into reality.

Phase	Need
Birth	Vision caster and catalyst
Formation	Organizer
Stability	Operator and innovator
Decline	Healer and innovator
Death	Chaplain

In the *stability* phase, the church needs a leader (leaders) with dual skills: operator and innovator. For the church to continue to grow, it must maintain (operator) what it is already doing well, while at the same time developing a new S-curve (innovator). When a church values stability at all costs, the eventual future of that church is to begin to decline (if it hasn't already begun to do so); thus, the church needs both an operator and an innovator at this stage.

Closer Look: *Which of these most fit your skills and passions: Vision caster, catalyst, organizer, operator, innovator, healer, pastoral caregiver? Which part of a church's life cycle would you most naturally thrive in? What other types of leaders does your church need to complement you at its current stage?*

A church in *decline* needs a healer and an innovator. Churches in decline are often churches in grief. People remember the days when the church was vital, when the youth would gather for dances in the parish halls, when the Sunday school was full, when the nave was full. Now they are faced with deferred maintenance, dwindling resources, and empty classrooms. The congregation needs a healer who can identify the stages of grief that they are experiencing. Many times a church that has been through major conflict will experience decline. Typically, this church will call as rector one who is skilled at healing but also get a maintainer rather than an innovator. They think, "if we can just get back to where we were, we'll be all right." But "where they were" was at the point just before decline began to set in. So, the rector who effects only healing in the congregation—and not innovation—may return the congregation to the previous place of stability, but the previous state was still one of decline. The church still needs an intervention to pull out of the part of the life cycle that it is in; that is, decline.

Finally, if a church is not able to be rebirthed and the congregation must close, the church will need a loving chaplain who will guide the congregation through the last phase of its life cycle: *death.* This is truly a death and must be treated with real sensitivity. A gracious memorial service should be held that will allow the congregation to celebrate its history and bring healthy closure to the life of the congregation.[4] Once the leader has an understanding of the appropriate size dynamics of the congregation and where it is in its life cycle, he can now turn to determining where he himself is as a leader with respect to his relationship with the congregation.

Chapter 3
Understanding Leadership

Leadership is not magnetic personality—that can just as well be a glib tongue. It is not "making friends and influencing people"—that is flattery. Leadership is lifting a person's vision to higher sights, the raising of a person's performance to a higher standard, the building of apersonality beyond its normal limitations.

—Peter F. Drucker

Leadership is ultimately about the relationship between leaders and followers. Effective leadership is not based on a written contractual agreement between the person attempting to lead and those deemed as followers. As this chapter will show, such an approach to leadership is really the lowest level of leadership. Max Depree says that leadership is an art; that is, it is more than a set of skills and more than being higher on the pecking order. Rather, leadership is really about the leader's willingness to lead and the followers' willingness to follow. The exercise of leadership is made up of a series of invitations to follow, along with attendant risks, and the willingness of others to follow and to accept those risks. The greater the risk, the more effective leadership must be. Consequently, the most effective leadership is a matter of the heart. To lead effectively, the leader must essentially lead people to a preferred future—a higher place that involves increasingly greater risk. They will not respond positively unless and until the leader first earns their trust at the lower levels of leadership.

Thinking Like a Leader

Leaders think all the time. They are asking questions that other people either don't have to ask or don't want to ask. Socrates was right when he said that an unreflected life is not worth living. But take that statement a step further: in parish ministry, an unreflected life is a recipe for disaster. As you grow in leadership, you will need to spend even more time in thinking and reflecting (and praying), not less.

So, how does the leader think like a leader? There are an awful lot of leadership theories out there. It is easy to keep oneself so busy reading about leadership that one doesn't really have enough time to lead. Here are some starting points.

***Closer Look**: Who are the three most influential people in your life? Why were they significant to you? How did they motivate you, through coercion or encouragement? How did you feel when it was all over?*

Transactional Leadership and Transformational Leadership

James MacGregor Burns makes a distinction between what he calls "transactional" leadership and "transformational" leadership.[5] Transactional leadership involves the task of getting things done. Followers will follow the leader because there is something in it for the follower. A transactional leader will encourage with statements such as:

- "Sell so many widgets and you'll make so much money."
- "If you will do this and this, you will be a success."

Transformational leadership has a moral dimension to it. It involves the leader tuning into the perceived motives of the followers and inviting them to follow based on higher motives and morality. Transformational leadership involves such things as vision, integrity, ideals, and values. A transformational leader will encourage with statements such as:

- "I know it's difficult, but it's the right thing to do."
- "Faith is the substance of things hoped for, the evidence of things not seen."

Two things are important to know about transactional leadership. First, it comprises the vast majority of exchanges between leaders and followers. This kind of leadership is based on mutual reward for both leader and follower. Second, transactional leadership is the lower form of leadership. It has no real moral dimension or sense of intrinsic right and wrong. It accepts the goals, structure, values, and culture of the existing organization. Transactional leadership works within the existing system to accomplish the goals of the organization.

The aim of transformational leadership is to influence major changes in the organization and build commitment for the long haul. Greater commitment among followers is fostered by means of commitment to shared values. Instead of accepting the status quo of the organization, through transformational leadership the leader aims to lead the organization to a preferred future—a higher level.

The pastor must be an effective transactional leader, first accomplishing many things and achieving certain successes based on the current goals and values and culture of the church. When the leader first effectively responds to the felt needs of the organization, he then earns the right to lead the congregation to a higher level—the transformational level. In fact, if the leader remains at the transactional level and never moves to the transformational level, the congregation will plateau and will eventually—sooner rather than later—fall into decline.

***Closer Look**: Reflect on the responsibilities you have in setting people to task. Why should they want to follow you? What preferred future are you offering them? What's in it for them?*

Four Essential Components of Leadership Thinking

The leader's task is really fairly simple: to solve problems in the organization. As we showed in the last section, the leader starts at the lower, transactional level of leadership and then moves to the higher, transformational level. His aim is to lead the congregation and individuals within the congregation to a higher level. That's what I mean when I say that the leader's task is to solve problems. Some problems will be lower-level challenges, and some will be higher-level challenges.

Regardless of which level you are dealing with, leadership thinking has four different components:

1. **Define the current reality.** Max DePree has said that the first task of leadership is to define reality. (By the way, the last task is to say, "Thank you." Don't forget to say it.)[6] So, you have to ask yourself and others, "What is happening?" Your ability to articulate the reality of the current situation will affect not only the solutions you come up with, but people's willingness to follow you, as well. If you paint a picture of current reality that doesn't make sense to them, they will follow you no further. Thus, it is important that you define the current reality in such a way that makes sense to your followers.
2. **Account for what is happening.** Or, how did we get here? Louis Leakey, the noted anthropologist, said, "The past is the key to our future." It is important to know the background of the organization, ministry, or program that you are dealing with. Knowing the seminal stories of the organization and being able to tell the stories will help people to understand both how they got to that place as well as their place in the greater ongoing history of the congregation. Placing them within the context of the salvation history of the church gives their individual role dignity, meaning, and significance.
3. **Knowing where the organization is headed.** It's not always so important to know exactly what the end result will be. Sometimes, God wants to do something even bigger than we ever imagined. Father David Roseberry, rector of Christ Episcopal Church in Plano, Texas, had a vision of a large regional church that would have 800 in attendance. In 1985 that was a big, almost grandiose, vision. The congregation currently averages 2200 per weekend in attendance. The future reality was even larger than this then-young priest's dream.

   The important thing is to give people hope and confidence in God's desired future. You may not know the exact destination, but you can be confident in the direction. In our home, we have a framed calligraphy of a quotation attributed to Martin Luther:

   > This life therefore is not righteousness
   > but growth in righteousness
   > not health but healing,
   > not being but becoming
   > not rest but exercise.
   > We are not yet what we shall be
   > but we are growing toward it,

the process is not yet finished
but it is going on,
this is not the end
but it is the road.
All does not yet gleam in glory
but all is being purified.

I once asked a friend if he had any leaders on his vestry. He said, "No, but a have a lot of characters." If you don't have a sense of direction in which to lead the congregation, the "characters" among you will set the agenda every time. If you don't know where the church is headed, it will probably go in the direction of the loudest voice.

4. **Make plans . . . and hold people accountable . . . and bless the people.** Finally, make plans based on the first three components. How will you remedy the situation? Many people are very good at identifying the problem. The day will be won by the leader who can determine the course of action that will bring about the desired outcomes. However, making plans is not enough. The leader must keep people on task by holding them accountable. Finally, bless the people and celebrate their successes.

***Closer Look**: If you were to leave your position today with absolutely no forewarning, how would the person that follows you begin to take over your responsibilities? Would she have to start from scratch? Would she have to have someone explain to her exactly what to do? How would she know what her responsibilities are and what you intended for the group to accomplish this year?*

Introducing Levels of Leadership

We now turn more specifically to leadership levels. These correspond roughly to the lower/higher transactional/transformational approach that we looked at earlier. Using these levels of leadership as a paradigm through which to understand the relationship between the leader and the followers is based on the conviction that in terms of leadership, "trust is the coin of the realm."

Basically, trust is earned. People will not trust you in big ways or for big risks until you have earned the right for them to trust you for small risks. How does the leader go about earning the trust of people to follow at the higher, transformational level? Keep reading, and you'll find out how.

The first church I came to serve when I graduated from seminary was a small church in a small town. As is true of many churches in small towns, they had not quite caught on to the liturgical renewal movement. One example of this is that when I came there in the mid-1980s, the altar was still against the wall. I graduated from seminary with the sense that if I were to encounter such a thing, my job was to get the altar moved away from the wall. (In fairness to my seminary, I'm not convinced that that is what I was told; however, it was certainly what I heard.) So, here it was: my first challenge. I could do something positive in the life of the congregation and in furtherance of some of the values that I had acquired during seminary.

So, I set out to do just that: namely, to move the altar away from the wall and thus introduce some liturgical renewal in that place. (If you detect a rather unhealthy and presumptuous arrogance in the tone of this narrative, you would be right. By my attitude, I was aiming to direct them and "enlighten" them rather than to serve them.)

I was told that I could probably get such a change accepted if I could get it past a certain parishioner: Laura. When I met with Laura, she told me something that I will never forget. She said, "I heard that you want to move the altar away from the wall. You can do that, because you're the priest. I'll tell you what. We've seen you priests come and we've seen you priests go. You move that altar away from the wall, because you can do it, and when you leave we'll move it right back again."

Laura knew much more about leadership than I did. Because I was the rector, I thought I was the leader. I had certain stated authority as rector by virtue of the canons of the church and my job description, but I was a long way from being the leader with real influence among the congregation.

Who was the leader? The real leader was a layman who had long, lovingly, and faithfully served that congregation. Using Arlin Rothauge's analysis, he would have been designated as the patriarch. When the patriarch of the church spoke, everyone listened. When I spoke, they thought, "Hmm, that's interesting."

The leader who wants to manage change *must* understand the level of leadership; that is, how much trust he has with both the congregation as well as with individuals. The person at the higher leadership level can attempt a higher level of risk than one can at the lower levels. Keep reading to discover how we accomplished this change.

Here is the most helpful analysis of leadership that I have found.[7]

In the description of the levels of leadership model that follows, the patriarch, Frank, was a level 5 leader. People followed him because of who he was. His life had been on display for that congregation and community for years, and he had been found trustworthy and true. They followed Frank because of who he was and what he represented. As a long-time and esteemed member of that community, committed to the church, involved in their lives, he had earned their respect, and he was honored, beloved, and respected by all. I was the temporary chaplain sent from the bishop to provide pastoral care ministry. People would follow me only as far as my job description—because they had to. They would not follow me beyond my stated authority. I had to earn the right to speak into their lives by earning their trust.

Was the attempt to move the altar away from the wall a disaster? No. God was gracious in guiding me through this challenge. I used my stated authority to help Laura understand the theological basis for moving the altar. Together we discussed church history, theology, and how church architecture has changed throughout church history to reflect changing theological emphases. Laura was an apt learner and became a strong supporter. Then, we collected money for the refurbishing of the altar in honor of Frank and his wife. Basically, Frank loved the idea; and if Frank loved the idea, everyone had to love it, whether they initially liked it or not. Such is the power of both a patriarch and, in this situation, a level 5 leader.

So, let's look at these levels of leadership. The most insightful description of the various levels of leadership comes from John Maxwell. What follows is my summary of what I have learned from Maxwell.[8]

Maxwell's simple, but often repeated, leadership maxim is: "Leadership is influence." Leadership is the ability of a person to cause another person or group of people to do things that they might never do on their own.

He helps people to understand the difference between the authority a person has by virtue of his office and job description, and the authority a person has by virtue of his personal influence over others, the latter of which he has earned.

Five Levels of Leadership

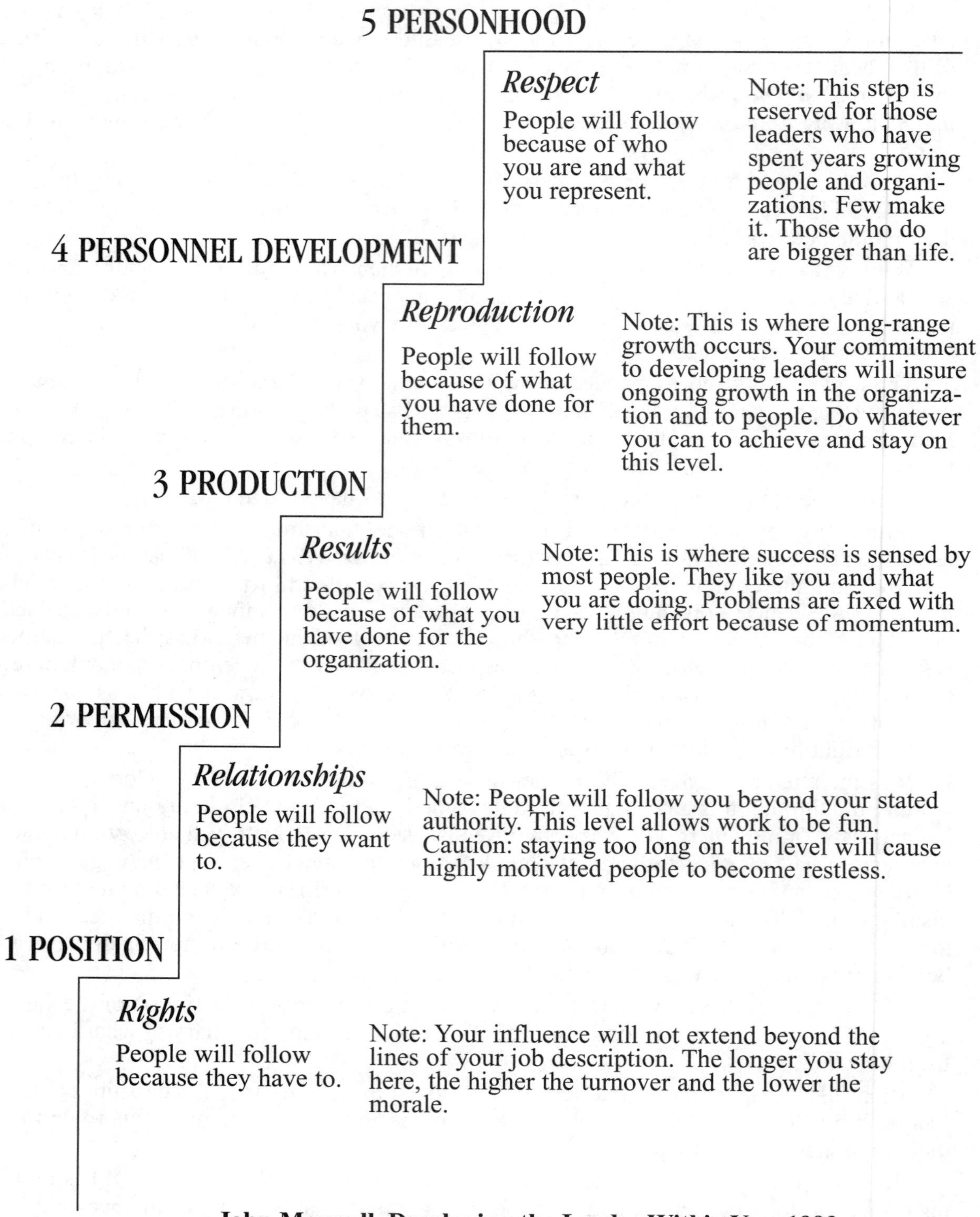

5 PERSONHOOD

Respect

People will follow because of who you are and what you represent.

Note: This step is reserved for those leaders who have spent years growing people and organizations. Few make it. Those who do are bigger than life.

4 PERSONNEL DEVELOPMENT

Reproduction

People will follow because of what you have done for them.

Note: This is where long-range growth occurs. Your commitment to developing leaders will insure ongoing growth in the organization and to people. Do whatever you can to achieve and stay on this level.

3 PRODUCTION

Results

People will follow because of what you have done for the organization.

Note: This is where success is sensed by most people. They like you and what you are doing. Problems are fixed with very little effort because of momentum.

2 PERMISSION

Relationships

People will follow because they want to.

Note: People will follow you beyond your stated authority. This level allows work to be fun. Caution: staying too long on this level will cause highly motivated people to become restless.

1 POSITION

Rights

People will follow because they have to.

Note: Your influence will not extend beyond the lines of your job description. The longer you stay here, the higher the turnover and the lower the morale.

John Maxwell, Developing the Leader Within You, 1993

Before exploring Maxwell's five levels of leadership, we will make a few comments to put these levels of leadership in perspective.

First, the lower the leadership level you are on, the lower the risk you can attempt among those you aim to lead. Leadership, and the influence that the leader has over followers, is ultimately about the ability of the leader to engender trust in himself on behalf of his followers. Trust is earned over a period of time. So, the more trustworthy that a leader is perceived as being, the more risks the leader can attempt. The lower the trust level, the lower the risk that the leader can attempt.

Second, you can't skip a level. The various levels build upon each other. Because they reflect the amount of trust that the people have in their leader, the leader cannot move to a higher level until he has earned the trust appropriate to the lower level.

Third, the leader will never be at the same level with all the people. He will be at a lower level with some and at a higher level with others. It is important for the leader to know at which trust level he is operating with which person.

Fourth, each respective level takes longer than the one below it. It can take about a year to move from level 1 to level 2 leadership and another year to a year and a half to move from level 2 to level 3 with the majority of people. However, beyond that, the leader must not be in too big a hurry. At these higher levels, he has to prove his trustworthiness, and that takes time.

How to Recognize a Leader

So, how do you recognize a leader? It really depends on what level of leader you're looking for. To identify the informally recognized leaders, watch people as you're gathered in a group. As people are involved in conversation, notice whom people look to when they talk. Where do their eyes go when certain people talk? Watch for body language to see who is listened to and who is not.

When you're working with a prospective leader, don't give this person responsibility all at once. Give him a small job. See if he fulfills his responsibility eagerly and on time. If he does not, don't entrust him with greater responsibility. A big part of leadership is delegating, not "dumping." Developing leadership is not about getting a responsibility off the leader's plate but delegating the responsibility so that it gets done.

Leadership Planning

Leadership is about moving an individual or a group of people from the current reality to a more preferred future. Because the leader is constantly concerned with the future that he is leading the organization or people into, it follows that the leader must constantly be planning.

The effective leader will consider various time frames of planning: daily, weekly, monthly, seasonally, yearly, and triennially (really). Although unforeseen events and emergencies always occur, effective planning allows the individual to handle those emergencies with less anxiety and greater confidence. Let's look at those five areas in reverse order.

Three-Year Planning

One of the truisms of leadership is that you can do much less in one year than you think you can, and you can get much more done in five years than you thought you could. To plan ahead for three years will of necessity involve other people in the planning process, but the effective leader will always want to have a general three-year plan in mind. There are some things in planning that you must set the foundation for today that will not come to fruition for three or more years. For example, in terms of vestry development, it will take at least a full three years—actually, four—for the vestry to reflect the vision and values of the new rector. Or, if the senior-high youth group is weak, energy and support should be poured into junior-high ministry, knowing that this investment will pay off in three years. At that time, the youth pastor can transition from a junior-high youth pastor to a senior-high pastor. Discipleship is a third area where the pastor must lay the foundation now for future benefit.

The three-year planner asks, "Where do I see myself/my organization in three years? What does that look like? What steps did I take that got us there?

Yearly Planning

The two most important areas of yearly planning are communication and evangelistic/gathering events.

First, in terms of communication, it is helpful for the priest to plan out a year's worth of sermons at a time. There are two primary reasons: one, to be sure that the larger parish *directional* issues are addressed throughout the year; and two, to address certain *individual pastoral* issues throughout the year. (Be sure to read the section on "The Difference Between Pastoral Preaching and Leadership Preaching" in Chapter 13.)

First, spend time articulating what you believe are the major concerns, direction, and goals of the congregation for that year. Then, use the calendar to place these issues within the appropriate context of the church year. Be certain to address such issues as moving into a new facility, focus on small groups, or the new Alpha Course, or spiritual disciplines, or a special stewardship emphasis, and so on. Next, I would be sure to address certain topics needful to be addressed, such as stewardship (not just in October but throughout the year), the Christian family, baptismal covenant, ethical issues, welcoming new babies into the church family, and so on. It's helpful to plan sermon series as a way of building a continuity of teaching.

Second, it is good to plan six or seven major evangelistic gatherings for parishioners to invite friends to and to build congregational fellowship. Some are built into our liturgical calendar, such as Easter, Christmas, Ash Wednesday, and so forth. Other special events can be planned, such as Praise in the Park, Friend Day (or Month), Patronal Festival Days, St. Francis Day (for the blessing of animals), Teacher or Police Officer/Firefighter Appreciation Day, and so on. Planning ahead in this way helps to begin to marshal the congregation's resources, not overtax them too much, and to space out the constant flow of invitations to the community.

Seasonal Planning

As you approach the individual seasons or sermon series, you can then focus in a more cohesive way on the sermon topics and the music that will engage the congregation. By breaking the year down in this way, you can give a distinct "flavor" to each individual season that can complement and contrast with other seasons and keep your worship fresh.

Monthly Planning

Plan monthly to help get projects done, plan for planning and retreat time, and make sure that you spend time with certain people that you need to spend time with. Monthly planning differs from seasonal planning in that monthly planning is for your personal calendar of priorities, and seasonal planning has to do with church emphases.

Weekly Planning

It is particularly helpful to plan the coming week in advance. The sample calendar that follows is a helpful way to view the week at a glance. This weekly calendar has sections for morning, lunch, afternoon, dinner, and evening. Write down on this calendar the various appointments and list the total hours each day that you plan to work. At the bottom of the page, list Three Major Intended Accomplishments. At the end of the week, list What I Accomplished. This will allow you to see the larger picture of what, in fact, you have been doing all week.

Clergy and other persons in the helping professions so seldom really finish anything. People's lives can never be broken down into short-term projects. Thus, it's difficult to celebrate any real closure. Writing down three major accomplishments each week allows you to have a sense of accomplishment and recognize that real progress is occurring.

Weekly Planning Calendar

Planning Calendar – **Week of**

	Monday	Tuesday	Wednesday	Thursday	Friday	Saturday	Sunday
Morning							
Lunch							
Afternoon							
Dinner							
Evening							

Three Major Inteded Accomplishments	*What I Accomplished*
1.	*1.*
2.	*2.*
3.	*3.*

Daily Planning

It is hard to discipline yourself to plan your day out in advance. Although not very glamorous, daily planning will actually allow you to focus on individual tasks and identify the things that are truly significant and necessary. Focusing on one task at a time will prevent you from being distracted by the e-mail that comes in, stray pieces of paper laying on your desk, or the unfinished project that you just toyed with last week. In addition, seeing in writing what you've accomplished at the end of the day will make it much easier for you to tell yourself to go home and feel like you've really accomplished something that day.

Finally, if you are the rector or vicar of a congregation, put on your calendar a full day of retreat each month and a several-day retreat each year. That is just as much work on behalf of the congregation as is visiting parishioners, meeting with leaders, and conducting worship services. If you are too busy to take a prayer and planning retreat, you're simply too busy—and probably finding yourself less and less effective to boot.

Chapter 4
Establishing Yourself as the Pastor: How to Connect with the Congregation

People don't care how much you know
until they know how much you care.

What an exciting time for St. Somewhere's Episcopal Church! A new chapter in the life of the church is about to begin. St. Somewhere's has just issued a call to a new rector who will come in six weeks. After the initial rush of excitement and the prospect of new possibilities and ministry in this new place and of sadness at the prospect of leaving parishioners and friends with whom the priest's life has been intertwined, the question comes, "What now?"

What now for the new rector? And what now for the congregation about to receive their new rector?

What now? Yes, the priest will have issues to deal with concerning leaving her current congregation: whom do I tell first? How do I begin to tell my vestry, my congregation? What do I need to do to prepare the church for my departure? Leave well so that your friends will remain friends and your congregation can prepare for the next season of their life. The departing priest will have lots to do as she leaves this congregation.

However, this is a time not only for leaving well, it is also a time for beginning well as you prepare yourself and your new congregation for your upcoming life together. Now is also the time for you to lay the foundation for pastoring this new flock, praying for these new parishioners, and planning for the ministry and mission entrusted to the care of this pastor.

Regardless of the size of the church, people who make up a congregation do not call a priest to be the chief executive officer of the church. Although good management skills are important for the effective pastoral leader, people call a pastor who will love them and care for them. They may place administration high on their priority list of qualities of the rector; however, administrative skills come into play only after the new priest has established herself as their pastor. The saying is especially true in the church: "People don't care how much you know until they know how much you care."

Henri Nouwen says that the leader of tomorrow must be able to articulate the inner events of those who listen to the preacher. He says that preaching is "the careful and sensitive articulation of what is happening in the community so that those who listen can say, 'You say what I suspected, you express what I vaguely felt, you bring to the fore what I fearfully kept in the back of my mind. Yes, yes—you say who we are, you recognize our condition. . . .'"[9] A good beginning, wherein the new rector establishes that she truly knows them and loves them, will lay the groundwork for them to entrust to the priest their lives, their money, and their church. This chapter will show how a new rector can establish herself as the pastor who knows them and their church, and loves them and will entrust her with the deeper things of their lives. Go to Chapter 10 for the discussion on engaging with your new staff.

The Pastor as Missionary

So what now? How does a new pastor prepare herself and her new congregation for a good beginning of their common life together? She does this by first knowing who they are as individuals and by knowing their church's story.

The new pastor should see herself as a missionary to this new congregation and in a new culture. A foreign missionary receives special training before entering a new culture. The missionary must learn the language spoken by the people of the new culture as well as learn the new culture itself. The foreign missionary will ask a variety of questions about the people in the new area where she will serve before taking up a new assignment to be able to communicate the good news to them in a culturally sensitive manner.

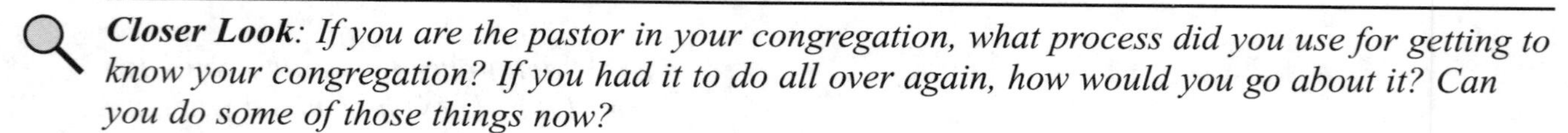

Closer Look: *If you are the pastor in your congregation, what process did you use for getting to know your congregation? If you had it to do all over again, how would you go about it? Can you do some of those things now?*

Likewise, the new pastor will want to know who these people are both as individuals and collectively as a congregation. What are their hopes and dreams? Their disappointments? What is their history? What is important to them as a group? Who are their leaders, and how has the church responded to those leaders in the past?

Learning the Congregation's Short-Term History

First, Look at the Numbers

One of the first things that a recently-called-but-not-yet-arrived pastor should do is to learn the congregation's short-term history. For the past 10 years, what has been this congregation's:

- Average Sunday attendance
- Membership
- Number of pledges
- Amount of pledges
- Operating income

By charting these numbers, the prospective pastor can begin to see whether this congregation is growing, declining, or plateaued. The longer a congregation has been at a certain level, the more difficult it is to bring about change. Here are some questions to consider:

- If the congregation is feeling positive about themselves, do the numbers actually reflect positive things, or is the congregation in a certain amount of denial?

- Do the vestry's and/or calling committee's comments about the general direction of the congregation comport with these composite figures?

- Can these numbers tell them something that they don't already know about themselves? or that they have been unable or unwilling to articulate?

Do these numbers tell the full tale of the congregation? Of course not. But reading them is like going to the doctor and having one's temperature, pulse, and blood pressure taken. They don't tell the whole story of a patient's health, but they provide a baseline for knowing where to inquire. Similarly, an understanding of the congregation's attendance, membership, and stewardship figures will go a long way in helping the new pastor to see the larger picture of the general direction of the church.

***Quick Insight**: Compare numbers of pledges with attendance and income. Sometimes, income may increase while attendance decreases, but no one feels any urgency because the attendance loss has been overlooked in the face of increased giving.*

Reading the History

The prospective pastor should also read the vestry minutes for the past three years, the parish newsletters for the past five years, and the annual parish meeting report for the past ten years.

The vestry minutes can tell the new pastor several things.

- What is the spirit of cooperation among the vestry?

- How has the vestry dealt with congregational issues?

- What is the commitment level of vestry members?

- When decisions are made, who follows through? Or are decisions made for which there has been no implementation?

Vestry minutes can further tell the new pastor who has resigned from the vestry or staff during the past several years.

- Who are the leaders on the vestry?

- What seems to capture the attention of the vestry?

- What congregational issues, problems, or celebrations came before the vestry?

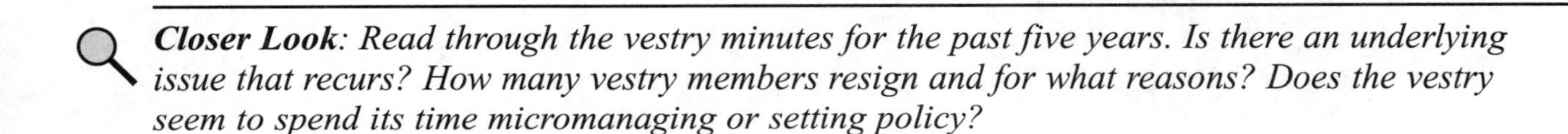

***Closer Look**: Read through the vestry minutes for the past five years. Is there an underlying issue that recurs? How many vestry members resign and for what reasons? Does the vestry seem to spend its time micromanaging or setting policy?*

A careful reading of the vestry minutes can be a healthy check on the search committee's or vestry's descriptions of the church. Also, knowing the vestry history tells the vestry that the new pastor knows their story, cares enough about them to learn their history, and plans to bring continuity from the past to the present.

***Quick Insight:** The new pastor can "score some points" with the new vestry by calling the vestry to implement or fund something that they had previously agreed to do but had never done.*

What can reading the parish newsletter for the past five years tell? Reading the newsletter can tell the prospective pastor several things. First, compare the newsletter five years ago with the most recent newsletters. Have there been any changes? Improvements? What is the quality of the design? Has there been a turnover in editors? If so, why?

What have been major issues facing the congregation as indicated by the newsletters? How have they addressed them officially? Compare the newsletters of similar months from successive years. Are programs consistent? Is there a consistency in the names of staff members and major ministry leaders? Is there a high turnover in volunteer leaders? Does the church try new programs? Is there any creativity? How many programs have been cancelled due to lack of interest? Whose names seem to appear in the newsletter on a consistent basis? Why? What pastoral issues does the newsletter reveal? Is the anniversary of the death of a child or the death of a loved one coming up in your parish family?

Finally, read the annual parish meeting report for the past ten years. What has been the official history of this congregation? Can you tell a ten-year story of the church from reading the Annual Parish Meeting Report? What are the strongest ministries of the church? Were any major initiatives announced that were not followed through? Reading this report will give the new rector a working knowledge of the direction of the church and insight into some of the major issues that will influence the future direction of the church.

***Quick Insight**: If the congregation doesn't have any past annual parish meeting reports, it tells you that they are probably a more oral-tradition rather than written-tradition congregation. This will help you to know how the congregation has typically communicated and an obvious possible way to improve communications.*

Getting to Know the Congregation and Staff

Learning Photos and Names

Coming to a new congregation involves a tremendous amount of change: new parishioners, new information, new neighbors, new businesses, and so on. With this barrage of new information to process, it's awfully difficult to absorb all of this new information. There are few things so important to parishioners than for them to feel that their new pastor recognizes them and knows their name.

A great way to establish oneself as their pastor is for the new priest to learn the names and faces of as many people as possible before she arrives. Immediately upon accepting the call to become the new rector of the new congregation, the new rector should have some people in the congregation take snapshots of individual parishioners and families after Sunday services for three weeks. The parishioners should take these photos with either an instant camera or digital, put the names of the individual parishioners on the back of the photos, punch holes in each picture, attach these with a ring, and send them to the new rector each week. The rector should communicate that he is praying for these individuals by name on a daily basis until she comes to serve the new congregation.

***Quick Insight**: Consider this ring of photos of new parishioners to be your "rosary!" Carry it with you everywhere and use it to pray for them while you're waiting at traffic lights or standing in line at the grocery store.*

Several benefits will result from this: first, the new rector establishes herself as a person of prayer—which is a very reassuring thing in a pastor. Second, immediately upon her arrival, she already knows many people by name and by face. People feel more significant if they are known by name. Third, the transition and incorporation process is made easier for the new rector because she already knows many of her flock. And, fourth, her new parishioners get prayed for by their pastor, and the congregation benefits spiritually from such pastoral care.

Writing Notes to the New Rector

Also, immediately upon accepting the call to the new parish, the new rector's home mailing address can be published in the parish newsletter. Parishioners should be encouraged to write notes to the new rector and her family, welcoming them to their new parish family and writing of some of their hopes and dreams for the congregation. This also allows the new pastor to connect with his new flock and to have an understanding of how to pray for them. Also, the new rector should respond, in writing, to each written communication.

Meeting the Congregation Through Small-Group Gatherings

An excellent way for the new rector to connect with her new parishioners is through small-group gatherings. Once the new rector arrives, arrange for a series of small coffee and dessert gatherings in the homes of parishioners with a group of 12 to 15 church members. Schedule these for the first several weeks of the pastor's arrival until everyone who wants to meet the new rector on this informal basis can do so. In addition, before each gathering, the pastor should be given the names and some information on each parishioner so she can engage in meaningful conversation with each one. Knowing your parishioners' names at their first meeting will impress them with your care and raise your esteem in their eyes.

At these gatherings, the new rector should not ask questions such as, "What are your hopes and dreams for the church?" or "What is your vision for the congregation?" She should tell them her own spiritual journey, sharing stories that will give them some insight into her life as an individual and as a pastor. The rector is laying the foundation for the kind of healthy disclosure that will build community at a later time. She will want them to be sharing their own spiritual journey in other gatherings.

Also, she should ask them questions that allow the new rector to get to know them. Four such questions to ask at these gatherings are:

- What is your name?
- Tell me a little about your family.
- How long have you been at and how did you come to St. Somewhere's?
- What keeps you coming to St. Somewhere's?

By the time the pastor will have prayed for her parishioners individually and met with them in these small-group gatherings, the majority of parishioners will feel as though they have connected with their new rector, and she will have gone a long way in establishing herself as their pastor.

Connecting with the Connectors in Your First Two Months

Although the new rector wants to establish herself as the pastor of the congregation, she also needs to connect with the leaders and influencers of the congregation. She will begin to learn which voices to weigh more heavily. Before she arrives and within the first week, she should ask the wardens and selected members of the vestry and search committee for the names of the top five people in the parish and in the community that they think she should visit. These would be people of influence, knowledge, or simply good connections in the church and community. Also, there might be persons particularly beloved in the church that ought to be visited. With people within the parish, ask about that person's history in the parish, what they see as the major issues, turning points, challenges, and so on, in the life of the congregation (if this person has already been met in one of the small-group gatherings; otherwise, be sure to get to know *them* as individuals first). In addition, these people should be asked for a list of three to five people that the new rector ought to visit within the first six weeks. (It is important that the priest not promise to make an appointment with each of these persons; she is simply making such a list and will determine whom she should actually visit. She is simply trying to prioritize her initial visits.)

Chapter 5
Discerning Your Congregation's Genesis Story to Further the Mission of the Church

[Joshua] said to the Israelites, "In the future when your descendants ask their fathers, 'What do these stones mean?'"

—Joshua 4:21

Once the new pastor has spent his first several weeks listening to individuals and their stories, he should then go to the next level: elicit and listen to the stories of the congregation as a congregation.

In order for the new pastor of a congregation to establish himself as the pastor to individuals in his congregation, he must spend time with them, hearing their stories, getting to know them, and gaining insight into their lives as individuals. The same is true of the relationship between the pastor and his congregation as a whole congregation. The congregation is essentially a person with its own story as well. Not only must the new pastor be conversant with the stories of individual persons, he must also be conversant with the congregation's story.

One of the challenges of a new pastor is to understand the history of his church as an institution, not simply who the previous pastors were and when certain building were built. He will want to know his congregation's life story. Knowing the size of the congregation and understanding the dynamics of its particular size is part of the process. Also, discerning where the congregation is in terms of its congregational life cycle is crucial for the pastor in knowing whether to emphasize vision or revisioning in his overall direction of the congregation. But the congregation has a story of its own. Out of the birth-growth-plateau-decline life cycle emerges a series of stories that has shaped that congregation and has shaped its members. This is the corporate memory of the congregation. The effective pastor will be both a keeper of the congregation's stories and the storyteller of the corporate memory of the congregation.

To learn that life's story, the pastor must start with discerning his congregation's Genesis story.

What Is a Genesis Story?

What is a Genesis story? When I was in seminary, my Old Testament professor spent nearly all of the first semester on the book of Genesis (this was 12 hours of class time per week, so we got to know the book of Genesis intimately). He spent so much time on Genesis, he said, because in order for you to understand the rest of the Bible, you have to understand Genesis.

The name *genesis* means "beginning." The book of Genesis contains stories of beginnings: the beginning of creation, earth, humanity, community, sin, cultures, languages, and so on. The stories of Genesis contain the seminal pattern for all of salvation history: creation, fall, judgment, and redemption. By understanding these stories from Genesis and discerning the pattern of God's dealing with his people, the student of the Bible will then begin to see this pattern emerge throughout the scriptures. He will begin to see that history is not just a series of random events. Rather, he will begin to view history through the eyes of faith and see God's hand at work in history so that it is no longer simply history but salvation history that he is witnessing.

Similarly, a congregation's Genesis story is a story that reveals the God-implanted motivation that the people who established the congregation had when they began that congregation. In truth, it is not their vision; it is the vision that God implanted in their souls. The Genesis story bears within it the vision of the congregation that is borne in the corporate soul of the congregation from generation to generation. The vision of the congregation is what has drawn people to that congregation year after year.

Understanding and living into that God-implanted vision is key to the healthy future development of the congregation.

***Closer Look**: Look at the buildings and rooms and memorial plaques around the church. Which names repeat themselves? Particularly know the stories of those for whom buildings and rooms are named. Are some of those families still a part of the congregation?*

America's Genesis Story

The United States of America has a Genesis story. This story is read and told to schoolchildren from generation to generation. Part of its Genesis story is reenacted year after year at school pageants. By knowing this Genesis story through rehearing and reexperiencing, millions of developing Americans learn the values that made this country what it is and the values that her elders wish to inculcate in the souls of her citizenry.

Why do more than a million legal and illegal immigrants come to this country each year? Remember the story of the Pilgrims? These more recent immigrants come to these shores for the same reason that those early Pilgrims came to America: for freedom, both economic and religious.

Recall the story of George Washington. Young George was asked by his father if he had used his hatchet to chop down a cherry tree. His famous reply was, "Father I cannot tell a lie. I cut down the tree."

The story of George Washington chopping down the cherry tree was invented by Parson Mason Locke Weems, who related it in a biography published a few years after Washington's death. This story of the "father of our country" has illustrated for generations of Americans the importance of honesty and bravery as values for all Americans to embrace.

These two stories from the early years of this country communicate the core values of this country. America is the "land of the free and the home of the brave." Each year brings new immigrants to the shores of this land of opportunity. As long as America protects freedom, lives up to her responsibilities with bravery, and provides further opportunities for her citizens and immigrants, succeeding generations will continue to flock to this country.

In the same way, God implants a divine purpose in the corporate soul of each congregation. The local Episcopal Church is not simply the local franchise operation of our denominational brand, the "Episcopal presence in this community." Rather, God has given each congregation a distinct purpose, a unique DNA of which Anglican identity and ethos are only one part. As the congregation affirms and lives into that purpose, it helps to align the congregation according to its past so that it can move in a connected way into the future and fulfill the very purpose for which God called that congregation into being.

***Quick Insight**: Why was your church started? What were the hopes, dreams, and aspirations of its founders? What stories from those early days will give you insight as to what God had in mind when your congregation was planted?*

Wise pastors and leaders will work to discern the divine purpose for their congregation. This comes through hearing the stories of the congregation with discerning ears. As the leaders begin to understand and are able to articulate the core values of their congregation, they will be able to align the ministries in such a way as to fulfill the vision of the congregation that is borne by the corporate soul of the congregation.

Some Examples

Here are two Genesis stories that I encountered in my years as a parish priest.

The first congregation was in a small-town setting picturesque enough to be a popular tourist town. When I was called to serve this church, it had been in existence for more than thirty years and was fairly comfortable with itself. After many years of mission status, the congregation had achieved parish status ten years earlier,[10] their finances were in good shape, and the facilities were in excellent condition: by most measures of success in our denomination, this church was successful. The general belief was that if the church would just continue what it had been doing, the church would be just fine. It had reached a place of comfortable stability.

The congregation was content to do social-needs outreach in the community to fulfill its call to mission. What I discovered as I read the history of the church and listened to the stories of the long-term members is that the church was founded by "outsiders" to this community who were not members of the dominant ethnic group. By the time I arrived, it had lost its vision for welcoming the newcomer and was being strongly influenced by a certain "in group" who were happy to see things remain as they had been.

In my preaching, I would tell stories about the early days of the church, where they met, and who some of those early pioneers were. We identified the church's special calling as a church that welcomed newcomers to our community. We also identified the primary spiritual gifts of my two predecessors. The first was heavily involved in social action. The second was a deeply spiritual person. My gift as pastor of the congregation was recognized as evangelism. We saw the first two rectors as providing foundational gifts for the health of the church. Now it was time to welcome the newcomers among us and to make a place for them in our common life. As we began to welcome newcomers and identified our evangelistic efforts as bringing in the outsiders—just as many members of the congregation were considered outsiders to a certain segment of our community—the majority of the congregation welcomed the new efforts.

The average Sunday attendance of this church grew 32 percent in three years as they embraced their Genesis story and truly lived into the divine purpose for which God called them into being.

Another congregation had a similar story. This church was about fifty years old and had grown slowly over the years. Under a previous rector, their Sunday attendance had hit two previous high points. When I arrived, the church had been without a rector for more than two years; they were in decline and were deeply concerned whether they would "ever grow again." They had paid off their mortgage several years ago during the tenure of the previous rector but had engaged in no new ministry endeavors. Although they had had a history of involvement in the social concerns of the community, they had a more short-term history of curtailing their social outreach involvement and were now in an emotional decline and experiencing financial shortfalls in income.

I listened to people tell stories of the congregation's life, read as much history of the church as I could, and discerned what I believed was their spiritual gift as a congregation. The various stories that I read and heard told me that they had a strong motivational gift of compassion. Through the years, people were drawn to this church by their caring for others; people sensed that this was an inviting church that reached out to others. This spiritual gifting of the church was expressed through evangelism and missions and social outreach.

Immediately before I came to serve as rector of the congregation, the vestry had cut all outreach funds from the budget because of their financial difficulties. This was having a devastating effect on the emotional spirit of the congregation. I heard stories of the days when the church had done so many good things in the community. Deleting outreach funds from the budget was the *coup de grâce* of the congregation's decline. As I began to understand what I believed the spiritual gifting of that congregation to be, I realized the emotional damage that the cutting of those funds had on the soul of the congregation! For the church to be healthy, I knew that we needed to realign the ministry of the church with that gift of compassion.

The church was still experiencing financial difficulties. So, at this time, the church could not really afford to set aside operating income for outreach ministries. Yet, we couldn't afford not to be involved in outreach. I believed that we had to highlight the church's involvement in outreach ministries without being able to fund any ministries at this time. We did several things:

- First, we began to highlight the missionary efforts of some of our parishioners by including them in the prayers of the people while they were gone and having them share about their trips upon their return.
- Second, we highlighted the outreach ministries that parishioners were involved in throughout the community—we sent the message that even though we weren't sending money at that time, we were giving something even more precious: ourselves.

- Third, we began an evangelistic program that brought many new people into the congregation. The program we chose was the Alpha Course, and we committed ourselves to conduct five Alpha Courses. The net result was that people subconsciously began to sense that the church was living out its purpose. Although we had a vision and mission statements, no one could remember them. However, as we engaged in ministries that were in keeping with the Genesis story of the congregation and its discerned spiritual gifts, the congregation intuitively sensed that we were fulfilling our purpose as a church. Consequently, we arrested the decline and the church began to thrive.

How to Discern Your Congregation's Genesis Story

Discerning your congregation's Genesis story calls for you to become a sort of social historian of the life of the congregation. Here are some ways. First, *read through whatever archives, scrapbooks, and files* of newspaper clippings or photographs that the church might have from its history. Records of memorial gifts can also turn up helpful information or provide clues that the pastor will want to ask about as he interviews people. Second, *spend time with long-standing members* of the congregation and let them give you an oral history of the church. Third, *gather the senior wardens* (head of the lay governing board) who are still members of the congregation for a dinner within the first month of the beginning of the new pastorate. Call it a "Gathering of Eagles." Honor them for their faithfulness and sacrifice. Often, the burden borne by senior wardens is second only to that of the rector or vicar. Ask them to relate the history of the congregation during their year or years. Order nice ink pens to give as *gifts of appreciation to these servant leaders.*

As you gather, listen to these stories. Here are some of the questions to look for:

- What drew the original founders of the congregation together? What were their hopes and dreams? What amazing stories did those early church pioneers experience that could only be attributed to the hand of God?

- What were the church fights over? Chances are, those fights were over a disconnection between the vision of the church and how that vision was or was not being lived out. Look beyond the church conflict and you'll probably find the church's vision peeking out.

- What were some of the ministries that the church used to do that it is no longer doing for which there is a sense of loss among the congregation? The issue here is not to reproduce those ministries, *per se*, but to discern why those ministries gave meaning to the congregation and what similar ministries can you begin that will capture that same spirit—and calling.

- What were the "glory days" of the congregation? That is, when was the church most fully the church? That will give a sense of the congregation's self-understanding.

- Who are the congregational heroes often mentioned? What qualities did they embody? Were some of those qualities more appropriate for the church as it was then and not so much now? Can you detect a progression in the shift in the values that the church has honored over the years?

Telling the Stories to Serve the Vision

It's not enough simply to know these stories. The person who knows these stories and tells them has the power to influence the direction of the congregation. The telling and retelling of these stories shapes the corporate memory of the congregation.

The effective leader will tell these stories in a variety of settings in service of the vision of the church to allow people to "connect the dots" and be able to understand and articulate the larger identity and vision of the church. Effective storytelling in this way allows the congregation to identify its own salvation history and reveal God's movement in its own story. Telling stories that reflect and illustrate the vision of the church encourages people to reflect on their own personal stories and help them to identify their own place and purpose in the present and future of the congregation. This helps them to understand that their ministry is not just a generic ministry but is raised to a higher level: it is part and parcel of their congregation's unique salvation history and divine purpose.

Thus, it is important for the pastor and other leaders to understand the congregation's story, character, and gifting. As they learn the stories and discern the divine purpose of the congregation, they can then tell those stories in service of the vision in such a way as to shape and affirm the congregation's self-understanding. Knowing the past in this way gives the congregation both connectedness with the past and an understanding of the purposeful direction for the future.

Section 2
Bringing About Change

Chapter 6

Bringing About Change (Without Wreaking Havoc)

You might be an Episcopalian if . . . the only kind of change you like comes out of a Coke machine.

There is no growth without change—whether the growth is measured in terms of numerical growth or spiritual growth. When it comes to churches, as the life cycle illustration from Chapter 2 shows, if a church does not develop new S-curves, it will eventually decline and die.

Just as there is no growth without change, not all change is healthy change. A bull in a china closet can certainly bring about change, but the chances are slim to none that it will be a happy change. This chapter deals with how to effect healthy change in a congregation.

Resistance Accompanies Change

The first thing that a person wanting to initiate change in a congregation must know is that for every action there is a countervailing reaction. Generally, people will accept small changes, but they will resist bigger changes. The bigger the change, the bigger will be the resistance in people. Generally, if there is no resistance, there is no change occurring. (And if there is no change occurring, eventually decline will set in. . . .)

A couple of examples will illustrate this principle. During the gasoline shortages of the 1970s, the Detroit automakers continued to make large, gas-consuming vehicles. Because Detroit failed to respond to American consumers' demands for smaller cars, Japanese automakers filled that void. Recently, Toyota became the number two automaker in the United States. Similarly, an alcoholic person will begin recovery, and the spouse who is used to having to overcompensate for the alcoholic spouse doesn't respond well. Because the spouse of the former alcoholic doesn't know how to deal with the newly found health of the person now in recovery, she will often "act out" to regain the attention that she was once getting as the beleaguered wife. This is called *codependence,* but it is also an example of resistance when change enters a family system.

Similar resistance happens in churches when significant change occurs that changes the dynamic of the family system. Such resistance is to be expected and even welcomed as an indication that change is occurring.

Maslow's Hierarchy of Needs

How many clergy have gotten in trouble with their congregations for attempting change before the congregation was ready for it? Or, how many clergy attempted too much too soon? Or, alternatively, how many clergy have sat idly by, maintaining the congregation, frustrated at doing the routine, believing that there really could be more to pastoral ministry than they are currently experiencing?

There is more. The right change at the right time can build momentum that will bring about more change. The wrong change—or the right change at the wrong time—can debilitate a congregation and frustrate the leadership. There really is a helpful approach to understanding what kinds of change a congregation can embrace.

The approach to understanding this kind of change comes by applying Abraham Maslow's hierarchy of needs to the congregation:

- Physiological needs
- Security needs
- Social needs
- Esteem needs
- Self-actualization needs

According to Maslow, the lower needs must be met before going to the higher needs. Similarly, in the church, the lower needs should first be addressed before moving on to the higher needs.

Physiological Needs

In Maslow's construction of the hierarchy of needs, physiological needs are the very basics of life and include air, food, water, and so on. These foundational needs must be met before we can go on to higher needs.

For the church, physiological needs would be such things as:

- Physical improvements
- Canonically required changes

These changes are easiest to make because they are the most obvious. When the pastor calls for cleaning, fixing, and painting, it communicates to the congregation that he cares about the church. Physical improvements tangibly foreshadow other intangible improvements in the life of the congregation.

Canonically required changes are also fairly easy to accomplish because we are a church under authority. The authority for bringing the church in conformity with the canons is not dependent on the authority or the discretion of the rector but upon canons whose authority is accepted by all.

Security Needs

Like physiological needs, safety needs also have to do with survival, but they are in some sense secondary, speaking more to safety and smooth functioning of finance and worship rather than sustenance. Security needs include:

- Safety of building, lighting, heating, and air conditioning
- Financial soundness
- Communications
- Scheduling
- Worship bulletins
- Worship service running smoothly

Changes to these secondary security needs may be a little harder to initiate than changes to more primary physiological needs for a variety of reasons. Solutions to security-need problems are less obvious. They are often more expensive. Also, they may impinge upon somebody's "sacred cow." However, successful changes in these areas reap benefits in the momentum of beneficial change in the life of the congregation.

Social Needs

Social needs refer to love and the need to belong. Humans have a desire to belong to groups, to love and be loved, and to be cared for. At this level, people are aware of their loneliness; and feelings of rejection and emotional hurt are preeminent.

In the church setting, this level of social needs moves beyond the mere administrative and survival functions of physiological and security needs. For most parishioners, the level of social need is the very reason that the church exists; namely, to care for the (pastoral care) needs of its members. Many church members resent it when churches seem to emphasize buildings and finances to the neglect of providing pastoral care for members of the congregation.

Social needs in the church that should now be addressed include:

- Pastoral care
- Connectedness
- Older members

When the leaders begin to address these needs, people will feel that the church is really being the church. This is what the "church is all about." Many family- and pastoral-sized churches stay at this level. It is impossible to move to higher levels of esteem and mission if this level of need has not been met.

Esteem Needs

There are two types of esteem needs. First, there are those self-esteem needs. These are derived from one's ability to master a certain task. The second type of esteem needs stems from the recognition and affirmation of competence or respect from others.

A church will want to deal with such esteem needs as:

- Reputation among churches and community
- Reputation in diocese and in the denomination
- The congregation's heroes
- Resurrection stories; that is, stories of the church overcoming major challenges

When the esteem needs of the church are met, it helps create a church where people find it easy to invite their friends. Members are proud of their church, and they want their friends to experience what they have experienced. The facilities are attractive; the ministries are done well; the preaching is excellent. In addition, their church is well respected in the community because their rector is involved in community or denominational activities.

Some esteem needs reflect the need for affirming connection not only with a church's larger community but also with its own past. Second- and third-generation church members will say, "My grandfather would have been proud," or, "Don't you wish that Mrs. Bessie could see us now?" Here is where churches are successfully accomplishing more than survival and the pastoral care needs of its members. When esteem needs are met, it communicates to the congregation that their church "is built to last."

Self-Actualization Needs

This is the highest level where the individual becomes all that God intended him or her to be. At this level, people are maximizing their potential. The needs for self-actualization are often expressed through music, art, poetry, and so on.

Churches as well as individuals have a need to fulfill their unique identity. Some churches are missions-oriented, emphasize teaching, excel in their music program, emphasize social outreach, and so on.

Churches respond to the need for self-actualization when they identify and are fulfilling their vision and expanded mission

The church at this level is able to expand beyond the nongeneric ministries of pastoral care, Christian education, choir, and so on. Although the church will need to be involved in missions and outreach at the esteem level, here the church can take on a very large undertaking that will call for great sacrifice—as well as great reward—on the part of the congregation.

Establishing Your Priorities for Change

Leaders confront two opposite dangers when leading a congregation. One danger is that the leader will make a change without doing the background assessment and laying the groundwork: Ready, Fire, Aim! The rationale for this approach is, "My organization is in trouble, and I've got to do something." Without having asked the proper questions, the organization may end up changing the wrong things.

The other danger is that the leader will appoint committees that do too much background assessment and laying of groundwork. They meet, do a lot of research, discuss things endlessly, finally prepare a report, and end up accomplishing nothing: Ready, Aim, Aim, Aim. . . ." (That's why task forces are preferred rather than committees. Committees tend to study things, whereas task forces are usually chartered to get specific tasks accomplished.)

The pastor that has recently arrived at a congregation will be tempted to want to talk about mission and all the new things that he wants to accomplish. However, mission and expansion of ministry are either esteem-level needs or self-actualization-level needs. It is awfully difficult to gain much headway at these higher levels without having first gained a lot of trust and credibility at the lower levels. Start with the tangible; once you have accomplished some credibility in the tangible needs of the church, people will then begin to trust you with the intangibles of their lives.

For example, one church I served had some trees whose roots were growing into the foundation of one of the church's buildings. Several years earlier, the church had hired an engineer to study the effect of the roots on the foundation. The engineer said that the roots were, indeed, damaging the foundation and would eventually cause cracks and instability to the foundation. He recommended that the trees be removed. However, the vestry thought that these trees had been given by a family in the parish and was concerned that the donors might be upset if the trees were removed. So, nothing was done for several years.

Shortly after I became rector, we established a task force to consider the five-year and long-term facilities needs of the congregation. As a part of their needs assessment survey, the task force identified as one of its action-items the long-forgotten trees whose roots were causing unobvious damage to the foundation. This task force researched the history of the trees and found the original engineer's recommendations. They looked through the files containing all information on memorials given to the church and found no records pertaining to the donation of these trees. Finally, they placed an article in the parish newsletter stating the engineer's recommendation, their concern that the trees not be removed without conversations with the donors, along with the request that if anyone knew who gave the trees and had objection to their removal, would they please contact the church office by the first day of the month. If no one came forward, the trees would then be removed for the safety of the building. The trees were gone within the month, and no complaint was ever heard. In fact, by their deliberate and decisive action, the task force was viewed positively as "really getting things done around here."

In our analysis, this is a level-two security need. It is one of those security issues that is not obvious on the surface and could potentially be expensive to repair. Once it came to the attention of a task force that was empowered to act, the problem was remedied. The removal of the trees actually enhanced the attractiveness of the grounds. The net result was that more progress was made on beautifying the church, and this added to the momentum of positive change during my tenure that later resulted in greater mission expansion.

Strategies for Managing Change

Often leaders will announce a change only to face an uprising of protesters. This is not surprising in a church that values tradition and stability. For some people, any kind of change is a threat. Therefore, it is advisable to have a strategy for accomplishing the change.

There was once a pastor who decided to move the piano from one side of the sanctuary to the other. When he did so, the congregation rose up in arms and demanded the resignation of the pastor.

The next pastor was called, and several years later invited the former pastor to assist at an anniversary celebration of the church. When the former pastor walked into the sanctuary, lo and behold, there was the piano—not where it had been originally, but on the other side of the sanctuary, right where the fired pastor had tried to move it!

"What happened?" the former pastor asked the new one. "How did you get the piano moved to the other side?"

"It was easy," said the new pastor. "I moved it one foot per week. After a year no one noticed that it had moved at all!"

Here are some strategies to consider when attempting to bring about change in a congregation. Sometimes these strategies will need to be combined with other strategies.

1. **Dedicate the change in the name of the patriarch/matriarch.** Recall the story in Chapter 3 about moving the altar away from the wall. The refurbishing of the altar area was done in honor of the patriarch of the congregation and his wife. This change was well received by the congregation because of the high esteem and love in which the congregation held the patriarch.
2. **Set a time limit for trial.** In one congregation that I served, our chapel seated only 18 people, with room for an additional 10 people in the back room—although those sitting in the back room could only hear but not see the celebrant and preacher. Our Sunday morning eight o'clock worship service was filled to capacity. We needed more space. We knew that that particular service would grow if there were simply more pew space for newcomers.

The congregation protested when it was suggested that the wall dividing the two rooms be removed to make one large chapel. This was a historic building, and this objection was not unreasonable.

We proposed a 6-month trial in which we would move this worship service to the main nave (sanctuary). If this worship grew to the size that after 6 months the people could not fit back into the historic chapel, we would remain in the main nave. If all those attending could fit back into the chapel, we would then move back to the chapel.

3. **Don't take away something without providing an equitable substitute.** Another part of the proposal was that for those who had a need to have Eucharist in the historic chapel, such as some of our long-standing members, we would add a mid-week Eucharist in that chapel.

   Within 6 months, the eight o'clock service had vastly outgrown the chapel. The original "eight o'clockers" accepted the change as being fair and settled comfortably into the service in the main nave where it remains to this day. The mid-week Eucharist was turned into a healing service that was preceded by some women of the church gathering on a weekly basis and praying for the church.

4. **Educate, educate, educate.** The importance of educating the congregation—or at least, those most greatly affected by the change—cannot be overemphasized. In the example of relocating the altar (Chapter 3), certainly the principal reason this change was accepted by the congregation was because of the affection that the church had for the patriarch. In addition, we had to educate the congregation in general but also two persons in particular: the directress of the altar guild and the niece of the patriarch (who also served on the altar guild). These two women were key influencers in the life of the congregation.

   Although they had affection for the patriarch, they were also the bearers of the local church tradition. To convince them of the rightness of this proposal, they had to understand the history and theology underlying the proposal. Once they accepted the reason for the change from a theological and historical perspective, they were able to support this proposed change among the congregation and assure people that it was more than just a "nice thing to do;" it was actually the "better thing to do."

5. **Pick your spokespersons.** When I first considered moving the altar away from the wall, I gave no thought to the real needs and concerns of the congregation. The woman who told me that "we've seen you priests come, and we've seen you priests go" taught me that I was a servant and a vessel called to serve the congregation and not just to manage the congregation. She also taught me that in most churches, clergy are perceived as outsiders with no long-term investment in the church or the community. Therefore, those proposals that had long-term consequences for the congregation had to be supported and led by the true leaders and influencers in the congregation.

   For example, it is generally accepted that the most effective stewardship testimonies are given by lay people and not by clergy. This is because clergy are expected to give sacrificially. Lay people do it voluntarily. Similarly, when a proposal has long-term consequences, the spokespersons for the proposed change need to be the most respected leaders in the congregation.

   In a parish meeting where we were educating the congregation about the need to buy acreage and eventually relocate the church, we had three presenters give reports from their respective task forces. One had been a member of the congregation for more than thirty-five years (and married to a founding member), one for twenty-eight years, and another for twelve years. All were well-respected leaders in the church and community. These persons totaled more than seventy-two years of commitment among the congregation. As rector, I made no presentation other than to introduce the three presenters.

6. **Use pictures to communicate your message.** As the saying goes, "One picture is worth a thousand words." Pictures can communicate powerfully beyond mere words. A church that wants to have a parish work day or do extensive repairs that will require the raising of capital funds can have a PowerPoint presentation that will allow members to see the needs in a way that no amount of words could describe. A church wanting to raise funds for a nursery, playground equipment, building for youth, and so on, can show pictures of the recipients and articulate how such an expansion could greatly expand the ministry of the church.
7. **Use surveys strategically.** A high percentage of clergy are intuitive. They will make decisions based on their intuitive perception of the situation. Sometimes these decisions are exactly right. When intuitives are wrong, they can be terribly wrong. Conducting opinion surveys provide two advantages as a strategy for facilitating change. One is that they provide real evidence of people's preference (as opposed to intuition and vignettes). The other benefit of using surveys strategically is that reporting the results and acting on them will engender support for the proposed changes when the congregation realizes that the majority is in favor of—or not in favor of—the proposed change.

   Be careful how the survey is worded. Never word the questions in terms of simply "yes" or "no." A better approach is to craft the choices in terms of a continuum such as "more likely" and "less likely." Be sure to solicit counsel from either a professional marketer or someone who has successfully conducted a survey similar to the one that your church wants to do.
8. **Know the seminal stories of the congregation and tell them in support of the vision.** The key to the future is found in the past. A church's past can inspire a congregation to engage in a challenge similar to the way that the church has responded in the past. Tell the "resurrection stories" from the church's history to show that as people of faith trusted God and God blessed their faith, so God will bless our willingness to step out in faith now.
9. **Establish your reputation for doing something really well.** Parishioners want to be proud of their pastor. No one can be good at everything, so if you as the congregational leader can establish your reputation for doing something particularly well, they will more easily forgive your shortcomings in other areas.
10. **Help people see God's movement in the life of the congregation.** When I was recognized as the evangelist who was preceded by the spiritually oriented rector, who was preceded by the social-action rector, members of the congregation were welcoming of the newcomers to the church and more readily accepted the changes that would help to bring them in. Because God had given me evangelistic gifts, we knew as a church that God would be sending newcomers our way, and we needed to be responsive to what God was doing in this chapter of our congregation's life.
11. **Change what is measured and what gets celebrated.** How does the church define success? New families and individuals in the church? New members? Greater attendance? More faithful giving? At each annual parish meeting in January, we would report on how many of our goals from the previous year we had accomplished and what goals we were setting for the next. Celebrating the accomplishment of goals helps build momentum for the congregation.
12. **Instead of merely thanking individuals for the work they have done, tell the congregation of one or two accomplishments or lives that were touched through this person's ministry.** Establish the "Second Mile Award" for the key man and woman in the congregation who went "the second mile" on behalf of the congregation during the year. Present them with a plaque along with their names engraved on a plaque hanging in a prominent place around the church.
13. **Bring in new people.** Consider hiring a new staff member, assign a current staff member to a new position (that he or she is passionate about), bring someone from outside the church to lead a vestry or leadership retreat or a short-term consult to deal with congregational

development or to study the processes in the church and make recommendations for changes. These kinds of changes can provide fresh perspectives not seen by people involved in the day-to-day involvement in the ministry of the church.

14. **Visit other churches that are doing things well.** Have your vestry and staff visit a church that is a bit larger than yours to learn how to function as a staff at a higher level than they are currently doing. We once held a vestry retreat at a church in our community that had just opened their new educational and administrative building. Just sitting in the new classroom encouraged our vestry to set higher goals for the upcoming year. Being there expressed a commitment to excellence that no words could adequately articulate.
15. **Last, but certainly not least, pray without ceasing.** Oswald Chambers says, "Prayer is the work." Prayer can accomplish so much more than planning, teaching, retreats, or dinners can ever do.

There is no growth without change. Change requires thoughtful and prayerful leadership. As the church grows larger, it becomes increasingly important for the leaders to spend intentional time reviewing, reflecting, praying, and planning.

Section 3
Working with Leaders

Chapter 7
Developing a Vestry That Makes People Want to Come to Vestry Meetings

If you don't know where you're going, you might not get there.

—Yogi Berra

The question for every rector, vicar, and warden in the church is, "Where do you want your vestry to go?" If you don't know where you're trying to take your vestry, you and the vestry might not get there. In fact, you probably won't.

Why? Because the dynamics of group life are such that, when there is no real leadership in a group, groups tend to move to the lowest level. Conversations in a group setting usually gravitate to the lowest common denominator. As we mentioned earlier, the Second Law of Thermodynamics would suggest that unless energy is poured into the system, what results is not greater order but greater disorder.

Most vestry guides deal pretty well with the functional requirements of the role of a vestry. The purpose of this chapter and the next is to help leaders develop vestries where members are effective both as individual leaders and as a leadership group within the church. Let's go.

Choose Your Mental Model

Building an effective vestry starts with developing the right mental model. What is the leader's mental model of what a vestry should be?

A mental model represents a psychological representation that the mind uses to understand real and hypothetical situations. A mental model is a sort of small-scale reality that allows people to anticipate events in order to give guidance for planning or simply for understanding.

For example, most people would agree that Western civilization has left the Industrial Revolution and entered the Information Age. Those are simple mental models that allow us to understand that we have left a time of using handmade tools and handmade items to the development of mass-produced power-driven machinery (the Industrial Revolution) to a period of rapid technological advance associated with the introduction of various information technologies (the Information Age). This is even after the period of time when the plow was invented, which brought about large-scale agricultural production and an agrarian-based society (the Agricultural Revolution).

Applying this mental model approach to a vestry, we see that different vestries function in different ways.

- Some really function as a rubber stamp for the rector.
- Others simply see themselves as a large finance committee.
- Still others see themselves as representing the values and concerns of the people that elected them.
- Some vestries function as the unpaid staff of the rector or vicar, carrying out programs and ministry of the church.
- Other vestries function as the board of directors of the church.

Your mental model will both shape your vestry and how its members relate to each other and the pastoral leader, as well as help you determine whether your vestry is effective or not.

***Closer Look**: Reflect on your last three vestries meetings. What is your immediate reaction to each of them? What specific incidents caused that reaction?*

We will see later that vestries will need to function in different ways based on the size of the congregation. Before we get to how to help a vestry function effectively, we need to look at the mental model of the vestry (which underlies its function).

The dominant mental model for the vestry in many churches is the institutional model. In this model, the church is viewed in terms of laws, procedures, and committees. Robert's *Rules of Order* is present at every meeting and governs the procedure of the vestry. This model understands the church in a top-down sort of way. The majority rules; the minority submits. This is representative democracy at its best.

The basic problem with the institutional model for the vestry is that it is simply not very effective in terms of real consensus and community building. The model is characterized by debating and voting; winners and losers; in-power and out-of-power. An institutional model breeds division both in the church as well as in the vestry as the majority gets its way.

An alternative—and healthier and more biblical—model for the vestry is that of a community of disciples. This model comes from Acts 6:2 where the early church had its first disagreement. Here, the Greek widows were being neglected in the daily distribution of food because the church had grown so large and the apostles simply couldn't get around to everyone. The resolution to the conflict was accomplished when "the twelve called together the whole community of the disciples" (NRSV) to address the issue. Out of this gathering of the community of the disciples, the issue was resolved and the church remained in fellowship with one another.

Moving from Solitude to Community to Ministry

Henri Nouwen helps us to see that ministry flows from community. In his article "Moving from Solitude to Community to Ministry,"[11] Nouwen maintains that effective ministry begins in solitude. He says, "So often in ministry, I have wanted to do it by myself. If it didn't work, I went to others and said, 'Please!' searching for a community to help me. If that didn't work, maybe I'd start praying." Jesus teaches us that the order is just the reverse. Luke 6:12–19, expresses the proper order.

> Now during those days he went out to the mountain to pray; and he spent the night in prayer to God. And when day came, he called his disciples and chose twelve of them, whom he also named apostles: Simon, whom he named Peter, and his brother Andrew, and James, and John, and Philip, and Bartholomew, and Matthew, and Thomas, and James son of Alphaeus, and Simon, who was called the Zealot, and Judas son of James, and Judas Iscariot, who became a traitor. He came down with them and stood on a level place, with a great crowd of his disciples and a great multitude of people from all Judea, Jerusalem, and the coast of Tyre and Sidon.
>
> They had come to hear him and to be healed of their diseases; and those who were troubled with unclean spirits were cured. And all in the crowd were trying to touch him, for power came out from him and healed all of them.

The order that Jesus teaches is: solitude to community to ministry.

Ministry must start with being alone with God, creating a space in our lives where God can act and speak. The solitude that Nouwen speaks of is more than just being alone in silence. It is being alone and listening in such a way that we hear the voice of the One who calls us the beloved. When we know that we are the beloved of God, we can walk freely in the world. Because we know that we are beloved, we don't have to prove anything.

Community flows from solitude. Community is the coming together of two souls who have both heard that they are beloved of God. In knowing that they are beloved of God, they become radically free, both to forgive and to celebrate: to forgive one another and to celebrate one another's gifts. If we have not heard the voice of God calling us beloved, we grasp at other people to satisfy our needs. We become resentful when others hurt us and jealous of other people's gifts and the recognition that they receive.

Solitude, community—then comes ministry. Ministry, Henri Nouwen tells us, is not something we do; ministry is the overflow of solitude and community. By virtue of being sons and daughters of God, and in radically free forgiving and celebrating relationships, healing flows to others. That is, in essence, ministry.

The Vestry as a Learning Community

The vestry is a community whose ministry is to lead the church. However, the vestry is a community with a very distinct purpose: to share with the rector or vicar of the congregation in the overseeing of the spiritual and material concerns of the congregation. So, what kind of community should the vestry aim to be?

The vestry should form itself as a microcosm of the congregation that they believe God is calling them to become. It is the conviction of this book that God is continually calling churches into the future to fulfill the divine purpose for which he called each into being. Organizations do this through nurture, fostering of creativity, encouraging new patterns of thinking, and where people are learning together. The most effective model, then, for the congregations—and, consequently for the vestry—is the learning community. The vestry should be continually learning as it expands the mission of the church and better serves the congregation. Choosing the vestry as a learning community for your mental model of what you want the vestry to be will change the way that vestry meetings are run.

***Closer Look**: How would you rate the energy level of your vestry? Hard-working and energetic? Taking care of business? Maintaining the status quo? Lethargic?*

How to Lead an Effective Vestry Meeting

I inherited the "approval of the past minutes, treasurer's report, old business, new business" approach to agenda making. If you want to have really long meetings, use this tried and tired method. Oh, and don't send out an agenda beforehand, either. Instead, hand out the agenda at the beginning of the vestry meeting; or, better yet, ask the vestry members at the beginning of the meeting what should be on the agenda for that particular meeting. This approach will guarantee a long and drawn-out meeting where much is discussed and probably very little accomplished. There is a better way.

What the vestry does at the beginning of the meeting sets the tone for the whole meeting. For example, the old "tried and tired" method places maintenance issues at the beginning of the meeting with approval of the minutes and approval of the treasurer's report. So, what you've done is devoted the most high-energy time of the meeting to the most low-energy issues. Also, when the vestry discusses the finances at the beginning of the meeting, you are telling the vestry that balancing the budget is really what is important in the life of the congregation. Most vestries, then, give their best energy and attention to the financial matters of the church and lose energy when it comes to the more important missional concerns. There is a better way.

Instead of the typical "old business/new business" approach, John Maxwell suggests an agenda with three sections: information, discussion, and decision. I have added a fourth, formation, and found this way of dealing with issues to be very effective.

1. **Formation** is the first priority for the vestry: being formed in Christian community. If your aim is to form the vestry as a community and further to form it as a learning community, then formation ought to be the first priority at each meeting. A helpful acronym for vestry formation is VHS: vision, huddle, and skill. I recommend 30 to 45 minutes for formation. Then, the business part of the meeting can begin. It is important that this formation time not be considered optional. Don't excuse people for being late on a regular basis. Formation is job one of the vestry.
2. **Information** is just that: information that needs no discussion or decision by the vestry, just keeping people in the loop. This section includes items such as new members, upcoming events of note, announcement of new staff members, or administrative issues. You're not asking the vestry to discuss or decide anything; you're just keeping them informed concerning what's happening in the life of the congregation.

3. **Discussion** covers those things where you want feedback or to do some brainstorming but about which the vestry is not ready to decide. I strongly recommend that nothing be presented to the vestry for an immediate decision without having been discussed for the month prior. To engage in discussion without pressing for a decision allows for a much freer exchange of ideas. People can discuss an issue without feeling the pressure of having to convince others right on the spot. Here, the pastor can elicit feedback on such things as the newcomer's ministry, the need to add another staff member, issues facing the congregation or diocese, or larger projects that will be decided by the vestry at a later date.
4. **Decision**. Only after an issue has been discussed by the vestry for the prior month should it be brought before the vestry for a decision—unless it is a "slam dunk," and there are very few of those. The presumption is that nothing is voted on unless it has been on the discussion agenda for at least a month. Generally, the decision part of the agenda will have the fewest items. You'll also find that by using this approach to setting the agenda, the decision-making items take up the least amount of time, because all of the discussion will already have taken place, and most of the energy will have been given to missional rather than maintenance matters. The wise pastor will know not to put anything on the decision agenda unless he or she already knows the outcome.

Another point should be made about the month (at least) between the time that an item is put on the discussion part of the agenda and the time for making a decision: the pastor should spend that month talking to vestry members, listening and addressing concerns, convincing where appropriate. The pastor should not miss the "premeeting meeting" where this particular issue is discussed. Again, the wise pastor will not put anything on the decision agenda unless he or she already knows the outcome.

Finally, after the teaching, sharing, or worship time of formation, after giving information, after nonhurried discussion about the life of the congregation, and after the usually nonargumentative decision-making time—now comes the treasurer's report. Placing the treasurer's report at the end of the meeting does several things. First, it emphasizes that finances follow mission and vision rather than determine mission and vision. This enables the vestry to focus on its appropriate responsibility as fiduciary agents on behalf of the congregation rather than having the financial discussions be the centerpiece of the vestry meeting and overshadow discussion of the mission of the church. Second, after spending all that time and energy on these other issues, vestry members are usually too tired to fuss much about finances.

The purpose of this approach is not to stifle discussion but to enhance it, not to hide information from the vestry but to make it more available. Think of the difference between an incandescent light bulb and a laser. An incandescent light bulb simply spreads out light in every different direction. A laser focuses and concentrates light to perform a variety of functions from pointing device to surgical incisions. Providing people with timely information and freedom of discussion without prematurely forcing a decision helps decision makers really process the information, makes them feel as though they've truly been heard, and ultimately draws the vestry together.

***Quick Insight**: What's the first thing that comes to your mind when you hear the term treasurer's report?*

Preparing the Agenda

Now, let's turn to how to prepare the agenda.

1. **The agenda and the treasurer's report should be distributed to the vestry members a week in advance of the meeting.** No new item of business can be placed on the agenda once it has been mailed out, unless it is an emergency (and there should be very few emergencies). Spur-of-the-moment discussions make for long meetings and can derail an otherwise productive meeting. Remember that nothing is put on the decision agenda without having been on the discussion agenda the month before.
2. **Individual financial questions should be addressed to the treasurer ahead of the meeting.** When asking a financial question, the guiding principle should be: Is this information for the good of the vestry as a whole, or is it simply based on my need to know or my need for clarification? St. Paul might ask, "Is the whole body edified by the question?"
3. **Prepare an agenda with clear time allocation.** As part of the agenda, make three columns: item discussed, with a brief description of what is at issue; who is presenting; and estimated time it should take. This gives the vestry a preview of the meeting and how long the meeting should last. It communicates that the agenda has been thoughtfully prepared and that they can expect a productive meeting.

Here is a sample agenda for a sample 2-hour 15-minute meeting:

St. Somewhere's Episcopal Church Vestry Agenda February 29, 2004 – 7:00 pm		
Topic	Presenter	Estimated Time
Teaching – "Sizing Up the Congregation"	Fr. Neal	45 min.
Information		
Approval of Minutes	Fr. Neal	15 min.
Staff Retreat – Wed., March 6, 2004; led by Canon Martin	Fr. Neal	
VBS Training – Sat., March 20	Fr. Neal	
Diocesan Stewardship Workshop, Sat., April 23, 2004 – All vestry members are expected to attend	Hunt C.	
Bishop's Visitation – May 26, 8 am and 10:30 am; Dinner with vestry, Sat., May 25, 6:30 pm – RSVP to Colleen B. Mission trip to Honduras – 23 from SSEC *– See handout*	Fr. Neal Fr. Neal	
Discussion		
Review of Newcomer's Orientation Process Recent changes to Newcomer's course, length, additions to process	Alethia A.	15 min.
Discussion of changing youth position to full-time	Fr. Neal	15 min.
Discussion of Whether to Host a Faith Alive	Fr. Neal; Tom L.	25 min.
Decision		
Land acquisition – Letter of intent to purchase two-acre strip of land across back of property *– See handout from January meeting*	Hylmar K.	10 min.
Aspirant for Holy Orders Chris Rocque seeks vestry approval *– See handout*	Fr. Neal	5 min.
Treasurer's Report	John M.	5 min.
Prayer		

Reducing the Time Spent on the Treasurer's Report

I've attended many vestry meetings where the treasurer's report dominated the discussion. We would spend so much time laboring over how much money the parish (usually) doesn't have that there was no energy for discussing mission. Financial concerns and debates will drain a vestry's energy for vision and mission. Moving the treasurer's report to the end of the meeting is one good way to shift the focus from finances to mission. Another way is to preapprove certain expenditures.

First, have the vestry authorize the junior warden to spend up to $1,000 on church-related repairs without prior vestry approval. The junior warden will simply report to the vestry about repairs made up to that amount.

Second, have the vestry authorize the executive committee to spend up to $2,000 without prior vestry approval. Again, the executive committee will simply report back to the vestry on such expenditures. (What is an executive committee? They are the rector or vicar, current senior warden, current junior warden, past senior warden, and treasurer or administrator who meet on a weekly basis to discuss the week-to-week operations of the parish.)

***Closer Look**: Review the minutes from last year's vestry meetings. How much time was spent debating expenditures under $2,000?*

Words of caution if you are establishing an executive committee for the first time: go slowly. Don't announce the formation of this group for the first time at a vestry meeting. Hold conversations with your key influencers to relate that you are thinking about this as a way of having a council of advice. Everyone on the vestry should be "on board" before the subject ever comes up in a vestry meeting. Some vestry members will eventually complain that a "small group is running the church" rather than the vestry. Return over and over to the larger vision of the role of the vestry, which is not to micromanage but to cast vision and establish policy to fulfill that vision.

Remember that vestry formation does not happen overnight. Also, vestry formation is not simply a matter of setting the agenda in the right way. What the pastor teaches the vestry and how she works with them in between meetings is equally important. To understand vestry formation, we have to understand that we are discipling both the individual vestry members and the vestry as a whole. The pastor will have to teach them how to be an effective vestry. The next chapter deals with vestry formation as a process.

Some people will complain that if the vestry does not approve those $2,000 expenditures without real debate, what will be left for the vestry to do? How about mission and prayer?

Chapter 8
Moving Your Vestry from a Micromanaging Vestry to a Permission-Giving Vestry

Don't spend 45 minutes on an $85 expenditure.

Neal Michell

Early in my tenure with one congregation, we spent 45 minutes of a vestry meeting discussing the pros and cons of whether to spend $85 on a certain item for the church. I had only recently come there and was still learning how the church operated. As the debate went on and on, I grew more and more impatient.

Finally, I pulled a $100 bill from my wallet (I usually keep one tucked away from my days as a lawyer when I might have to bail a client out of jail on a moment's notice) and placed it on the table in front of me. I said to the vestry, "I am buying this and donating it to the church, and I want $15 in change." I then proceeded to teach on the role of the vestry to cast vision and establish policy and not to micromanage.

This chapter will explore ways to turn the vestry from a micromanaging body to a vision-casting and permission-giving vestry.

Pastor as Chief Architect

The pastor of the congregation must understand that he is the chief architect for aligning the vision, mission, and strategy of the church. At times we confuse the servant role of the pastoral caregiver with the leadership responsibility as captain of the ship of the church. Particularly for clergy trained in the Rogerian ("what I hear you saying is . . .") approach to counseling, many clergy view themselves as primarily the pastoral care provider for the congregation, and their management role is fairly minimalist.

No one else can fulfill this role as captain of the ship of the church. We were created by God to follow a leader, namely, God. St. Augustine begins his Confessions, "Thou hast formed us for thyself, and our hearts are restless until they rest in thee, O Lord." Just as each human person has a God-shaped void in his or her soul that only God can fill, each of us is looking for a leader to follow. To defer to another this responsibility to be the primary leader of the church is to fail to live into our ordination vows.

Recall our earlier comments on the Second Law of Thermodynamics and the effect of entropy on organizations. When the pastor fails in this leadership responsibility, entropy sets in, and the vestry will gravitate to the lowest common denominator, which is usually in the area of finances. Similarly, when a group of people who don't know each other well are involved in a conversation, the conversation itself usually settles on the lowest common denominator of what everyone can find in common. It's called "cocktail party conversation." The architect of the vision, mission, and strategy will have to raise the level of conversation for the vestry. If he does not, entropy will set in, and the meeting will devolve to discussion about dollars and paint colors.

Teaching Your Vestry

Few churches provide orientation for new vestry members. Of those that do, often the topics cover the responsibilities as outlined in the canons rather than the responsibilities of the vestry as leaders of the congregation. Many vestry members have never been taught how to be an effective vestry. Bible studies and devotions and Eucharists before vestry meetings may seem like very spiritual things to do, but by themselves they are neither very efficient nor very effective learning experiences for the vestry as a vestry.

I encourage clergy to add monthly teaching components to their vestry meetings. Most of them object that there is so much business to conduct on a monthly basis that their vestry members would balk at adding another 45 minutes to the vestry meeting. However, if you approach teaching the vestry as an investment in their learning, the vestry will reap great rewards down the line. You may actually find your vestry meetings becoming shorter rather than longer.

Most new vestry members begin their time of service "baptized by fire." They are asked to begin with decision making rather than formation and orientation. Further, when they have no collective corporate memory, they have no history upon which to make wise decisions for the long-term benefit of the congregation. The result is that they have no plan to learn either about their organization, their history, or how to work together effectively for a common purpose. As St. Paul says, "how can they hear without someone preaching to them?" (Romans 10:14).

So, how will our vestries learn if they are not taught?

Taking Advantage of Teachable Moments

To move the vestry from micromanaging to permission giving, the leader must first be aware of and take advantage of those teachable moments that come along. A teachable moment is a time in the course of a meeting, a conversation, or a class when the hearer is able to learn in a new and fresh way. These might be called "Aha!" moments. Hearers get a new insight that they might not be expecting at that moment. Vestry meetings provide a regular supply of teachable moments.

The story of the $85 expenditure was a story of a teachable moment. I could have given a whole teaching on how the vestry shouldn't micromanage, but the experience of the frustration of the vestry in coming to a decision about whether to spend this $85 illustrated the principle in such a powerful way that it would not be forgotten.

The Old Testament prophet Nathan had a teachable moment with King David. David had caused the death of one of his officers, Uriah, and had subsequently taken Uriah's widow, Bathsheba, as his wife (who was pregnant with a child by David). The story of how the Lord sent Nathan to confront David with his sin is presented in 2 Samuel, Chapter 12. Nathan understood that King David had put to death messengers who had brought him good news; what might he do with someone who was going to expose his sin?

So, Nathan told his king a story about a poor man in his kingdom who had only "one little ewe lamb." This poor man had a rich neighbor who took the poor man's ewe lamb and served it to his guest. He then asked King David what should be done about this injustice.

The shepherd's heart of David rose in anger and said, "As the LORD lives, the man who has done this deserves to die; he shall restore the lamb fourfold . . . ." (2 Samuel:12:5,6).

Nathan recognized the teachable moment in his king's life and said, "You are the man!" David was able to hear Nathan's rebuke and repent.

As leaders, we must be aware of those teachable moments with our vestry to help move them to become servant leaders and permission givers to fulfill the mission of our congregations.

Annual Vestry Orientation

Crucial to the formation of any vestry is a time at the beginning of the year to provide an orientation for its members when new members come on board. This orientation should not be just for new members but for all the members of the vestry. We want each vestry member to be "reading off the same page."

Some previously oriented vestry members will complain, "I went to that last year." Good. They can help orient the new members. We are not just giving the new members information; we are forming the vestry as a community.

Some churches will begin the year with a vestry planning retreat. This is absolutely the worst time for a planning retreat. Why would we ask new vestry members who have not been formed, who don't know how the vestry functions, with a vestry that has not even been formed as a community yet, to try to discern God's direction for the congregation? A vestry planning retreat is better held in the middle of the year, after the vestry has learned, prayed, and acted together for 3 months.

A better approach is to begin the year with a vestry orientation retreat. This should be held away from the church and in facilities that are at least as good as your church has. I once held a vestry orientation retreat in the new educational and administrative facilities of another church. The excellence of their facilities spoke volumes to our vestry about the need for a similar level of commitment from our own congregation.

Four things should happen at a vestry orientation:

1. **Community formation.** Ministry flows from community. So, community formation is priority number one. Allow time for the sharing of individuals' spiritual journeys as well as their understanding of their own role on the vestry.
2. **Canonical requirements.** We are a church under authority: the authority of our bishop and of our national and diocesan canons as well as locally adopted policies and by-laws. The vestry needs to know these.
3. **Vision, mission, and values of the local congregation.** How would you answer the question of what makes this congregation unique? Why are you asking these good people to sacrifice their time, talent, and treasure on behalf of this congregation?
4. **The role of the vestry member and how the vestry functions as a group.** What are the roles of the different officers? Does the vestry operate by consensus or majority? Robert's

Rules of Order or a relaxed style? Are there attendance requirements, Sunday responsibilities, or liaison obligations?

I have found that churches that begin the year with this type of vestry orientation have a much more effective and harmonious year. I have further noticed that those vestry members that missed the orientation spent most of the year a step behind the rest of the vestry.

***Closer Look**: What do you spend most of your time discussing as a vestry? What would you like to spend time discussing?*

When planning for this orientation retreat, the leaders should ask what crucial issues are facing the vestry and the congregation. Have they already identified goals and directions that they want to accomplish in the coming year? This will give the content for some of the time together.

The Changing Role of Vestries as Seen through the Lens of Congregational Size Dynamics

Not all vestries are created equal. How one works with a vestry and how vestries function in a family- and a pastoral-sized church are vastly different. We saw in Chapter 1 that the role of the senior pastor changes depending on the size of the congregation. The same is true for the vestry.

In the family- and pastoral-sized churches, the vestry functions as the unpaid staff of the rector or vicar. These churches have few, if any, full-time or even part-time staff members other than the ordained person. Thus, vestry meetings function as staff meetings for the pastor. The vestry works with the rector or vicar to oversee the day-to-day operations of the church. Finances are often fairly limited, and the vestries of these smaller churches are tempted to micromanage. Vestry meetings are often concerned with the daily details of the running of the church.

Small Church Clergy, Vestry, and Staff Relationships

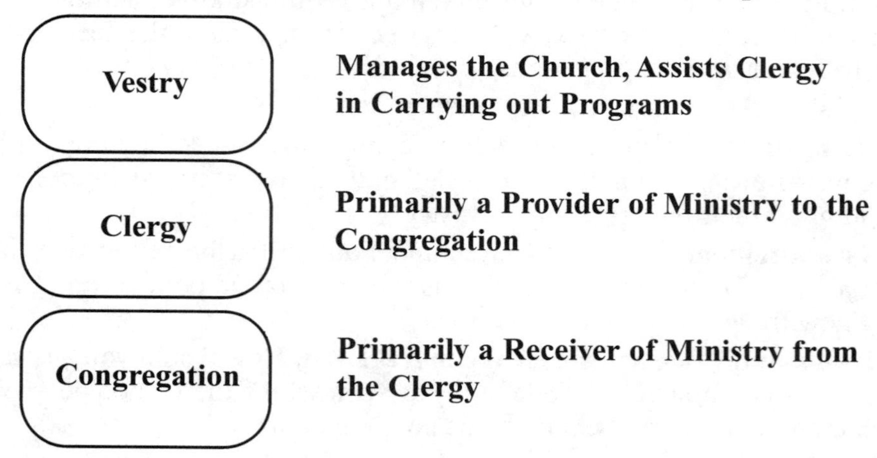

In an established program-sized congregation, the rector now has a staff to supervise. The staff guides the day-to-day operations of the parish. The vestry leads and the staff manages. The vestry shifts to more of a policy-setting role than the hands-on managerial function of the smaller churches. Operations flow fairly smoothly and require less of the hands-on assistance of the vestry at the smaller sizes.

Large Church Clergy, Vestry, and Staff Interrelationships

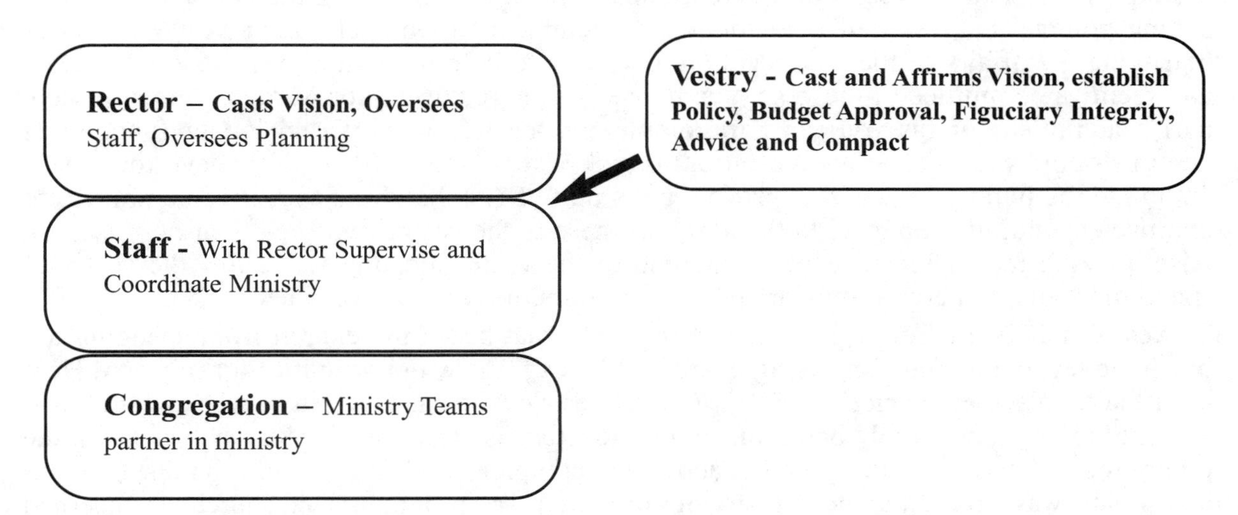

This explains why so many churches don't succeed at growing from the pastoral size to the program size. It's not a clean shift. The role of the pastor changes, and the role of the vestry changes as well. A management style that works well for the pastoral-sized church is ineffective for the program-sized church. As the church grows, what used to work is no longer effective.

This shift in leadership styles is accentuated in the transitional-sized church . The rector has to function as the pastor of a pastoral-sized church for 75 percent of the congregation and has to function as a program-sized church rector for 75 percent of the (emerging program-sized) congregation. The demands on the pastor are often contradictory and will cause expectations almost impossible for the rector or vicar to fulfill.

The internal pressure (to remain intimate, small, and not complex) of the pastoral-sized aspect of the church bumps up against the external pressure (to develop programs, ministries, and greater complexity) of the emerging program-sized congregation.

In the growth process from pastoral to program size, the rector cannot relieve this tension. The forces at work are really warring with each other. The rector must serve as the "non-anxious presence" in Ralph Waldo Emerson's poem, "If:"

> If you can keep your head when all about you
> Are losing theirs and blaming it on you. . . .

He must assure them that although the church feels unstable right now, this unstable feeling is normal for churches of this transitional size. The church needs for the priest to acknowledge and articulate the changes that are taking place and to guide them through this challenging time. The tensions and instability that people currently experience will be relieved as the church grows beyond 250–275 in average Sunday attendance.

The priest during this transitional phase cannot serve as the non-anxious presence alone. The church needs for the vestry, as the elected elders of the congregation, to be the non-anxious governing board of the church during these changes as well. They must acknowledge the hurt feelings and conflicting expectations that result from the changing role of the rector and the changing relationship between the pastor and the congregation.

Recommendations for Transitioning to a Program-Sized Church Vestry

A couple of shifts must take place for this transition to program size to occur.

1. The vestry shifts from the "unpaid staff" of the rector to a board that has two primary duties: casting vision with the rector and communicating that vision among the congregation; and setting policy. The vestry of a pastoral-sized church tends to spend their vestry meetings managing the affairs of the congregation. One way to help transition the vestry is to create an executive committee of the vestry, composed of the rector, senior warden, junior warden, parish administrator (as you grow in complexity, the treasurer can no longer function as administrator; you need someone on site), and past senior warden. Then have the vestry authorize the junior warden to approve repairs up to $1,000 and the executive committee to approve expenditures up to $2,000 and report these to the vestry (*not* seek their permission). Also, placing the financial report at the end of the vestry meeting will allow the vestry to spend more of its energy on vision, policy, and direction and less on finances.

2. The vestry must shift from a micromanaging body that keeps the church from spending too much money to a permission-giving board that looks for new opportunities for ministry. Here a shift takes place in the *modus operandi* of the vestry: whereas the pastoral-sized church was content "to be" (and simply being the church together is important for that size church), the program-sized church shifts to a more active and complex "to do" mode and so must be looking for new ways to expand the ministry of the church. The program-sized church is concerned with anticipating the needs of a newer and younger people through programs and staff development to create multiple entry points for new members.

3. The rector of a transitional-sized church must educate the vestry regarding the changes that are taking place in the administration and governance of the church. Thus, at this level, vestry education and vestry orientation become necessary components of vestry life. The transitional phase is full of teachable moments. Each month brings a change from the way the church functioned in the past. The rector must be diligent in helping the vestry to understand the reasons for the changes; the vestry will, in turn, also communicate these changes among the congregation.

In a church that I once served, the vestry had authorized the refurbishing of the children's nursery. We appointed a task force of women who were mothers or hoped to be mothers to pick the paint colors, carpet, and furnishings for the new nursery. One day, I went to the nursery to check on their progress and encountered a distraught mother. She was sobbing because one of the vestry members had told her that they could not remove the plastic molding along the base of the wall because the vestry made all decisions by consensus, and he would vote against it.

I had to assure her that, although the junior warden would oversee the work of her task force, the vestry had fulfilled their responsibility to the decoration effort by appropriating the funds necessary to redecorate the nursery. In doing so, they had passed authority to the task force to decorate the nursery in a manner in which they as mothers would feel comfortable leaving their babies.

Then, as rector, I had to teach the vestry that their job was vision, mission, and policy. This was a teachable moment at a crucial time in the development of the vestry into a mission-minded, permission-giving vestry.

4. **The parish becomes increasingly staff-led.** The rector must transition his or her volunteers into a staff. Because of the shift in the vestry to a more vision-casting and policing-setting body, at times vestry members will feel less busy and that their roles have become diminished when really the opposite is true. The hands-on involvement of the individual vestry members will become reduced; this must be replaced with the addition of new staff members. Many churches at this size are understaffed and as a result are subsequently staffed to plateau. The church must add staff strategically, not understaffing (which is often the case) and not inappropriately staffing (less often). Staff meetings, staff development, and staff planning are new skills that the transitioning rector must develop.

***Quick Insight**: Compare what happens at the staff meeting with what happens at the vestry meeting. What does this tell you about your church?*

---

5. **The vestry must shift to more of a task-force and problem-solving approach.** Rather than have ongoing committees (standing committees of the vestry), which are appropriate to a more stabilized congregation, the vestry will want to make more and more use of short-term task forces that focus on problem solving rather than the governing approach that committees and commissions engender. Staff will want to use advisory task forces, but these must work for the staff person rather than for the vestry person who serves on the advisory task force.

   The program- and resource-sized churches will have a more established vestry with fairly clearly defined roles. Here are the six roles appropriate to a large church vestry.

- **Nominations:** Look for people who are well connected among the congregation and teachable. Have a combination of long-time members and newcomers in the congregation to provide for the healthy transference of authority in the church to the next generation.
- **Personnel:** It is appropriate that the vestry assist with personnel review. However, the vestry should not insert itself between rector and staff and congregation. The rector must be allowed to supervise the staff.
- **Planning:** The vestry should have both long- and short-range planning committees. The church should develop a strategic plan for the church and revise it from time to time. Many issues that the church will need to attend to can be addressed by *ad hoc* task forces. Task forces are preferable to committees, because task forces tend to have shorter life spans and are more action-oriented than committees tend to be.
- **Budget:** Much budgeting preparation will be done by the individual staff members and their working groups. Although the vestry has oversight responsibility over the budget, it is important that they not micromanage. They should determine the minimum level of funding that they will concern themselves with and ensure that mission priorities drive the budget.
- **Policy:** The vestry in these larger-size churches will need to establish policy for the church that is in keeping with the vision and mission of the church. It is important when facing policy issues that the vestry anticipates but doesn't react to crisis situations. The vestry should never enact a policy in one meeting
- **Mission and vision:** Lack of clear vision and direction encourages conflict and micromanaging among the vestry as well as among the congregation. Budget and personality will

sometimes determine the program priorities of the church rather than mission. It is the vestry's responsibility that the program priorities fulfill the vision and strategic plan of the congregation.

6. **The rector, vestry, and staff understand that ministry shifts to laity.** This is one of the most difficult shifts to facilitate. Lay people who are accustomed to receiving ministry now become partners in providing ministry. Clergy and staff who receive their primary affirmation from how well they *provide* ministry must now receive their primary affirmation from how well they *multiply* ministry. The vestry must provide support for this shift when the expected "pushback" occurs from the congregation from this shift in ministry.

The Spiritual Level of Your Vestry

Building an effective vestry involves more than forming the vestry into a community and educating the vestry regarding congregational size dynamics. The pastor must also be concerned to assist the vestry in deepening their spiritual maturity as well.

Many times, churches have a desire to grow numerically without laying the spiritual foundation for healthy growth. Healthy growth starts with a spiritually healthy and maturing vestry. The number one responsibility of the pastor is to develop the vestry into a spiritually healthy community.

Why do I say that?

It has often been said that in a church, the congregation can rise no higher than the spiritual level of the priest. It is also true that the congregation can rise no higher than the spiritual level of the vestry. If the vestry is not at the highest spiritual level of the church, they will not understand the importance of vision, the deeper spiritual issues necessary to fulfill the vision, and will not stretch to achieve that vision; neither will it have the spiritual sustenance to get through the times of testing that come with fulfilling any worthwhile vision.

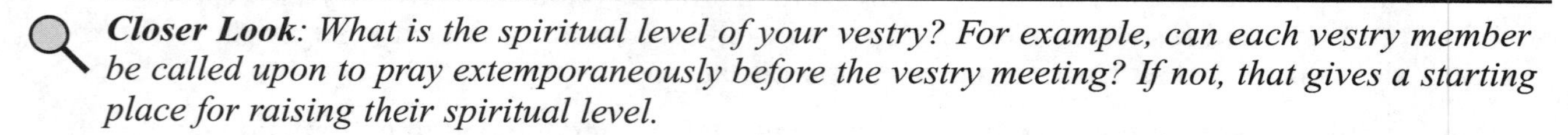

Closer Look*: What is the spiritual level of your vestry? For example, can each vestry member be called upon to pray extemporaneously before the vestry meeting? If not, that gives a starting place for raising their spiritual level.*

Various people have come up with ways of helping to measure spiritual growth.[12] The particular method of measurement that one uses is less important than that the pastor actually have some means of measuring the spiritual level of the vestry. As the saying goes, "What gets measured gets done."

Here is a way of measuring spiritual maturity:

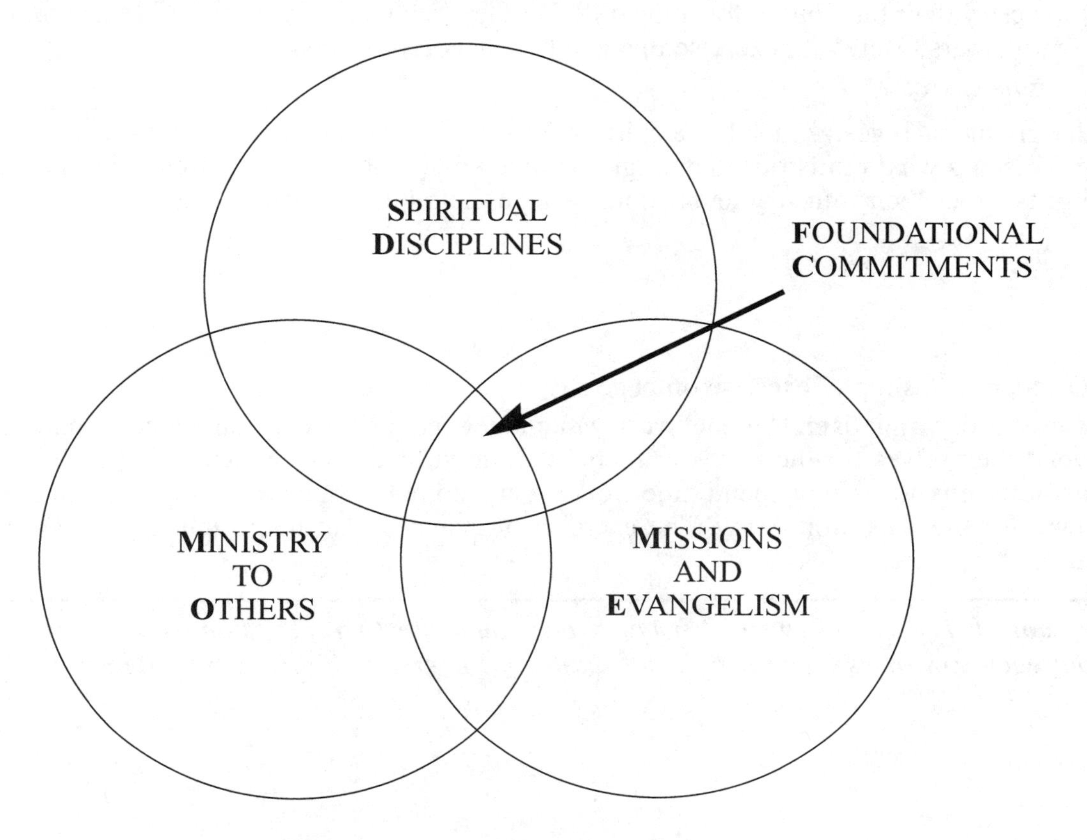

Measuring Your Spiritual Maturity

1. **Foundational commitments:** There are three that are foundational to serving as an effective vestry member. Commitment to Jesus Christ as Savior and Lord, commitment to the local church as evidenced by membership, and financial commitment to the church.

   First, can each vestry member articulate his or her faith? Can they give their testimony of faith in Christ in a five-minute talk? The exercise on page 79 can help accomplish this.

   Second, what is the level of commitment to the church of the individual vestry member? Has she been a leader in other ministries in the church? Does she have a positive view of the church and its vision and direction?

   Third, what is the level of this person's financial commitment to the church, not in terms of dollars, but is this vestry member's financial commitment commensurate with his financial ability to give? Are there stewardship expectations for vestry members such as tithing or proportionate giving?

2. **Spiritual formation:** Is this person growing as a Christian? Can each vestry member pray aloud and articulate the needs and concerns of the church? What are the highest expectations of commitment in the church? If a vestry member is not living at the highest level of commitment, how can he or she call others to commitment? What are the expectations of attendance at parish events and worship services? Daily office or quiet time or daily devotional time? Participation in a Bible study, small group, or Sunday school class? The exercise on page 80 can help highlight some of these issues.

3. Ministry to others: What is the level of involvement of the vestry members outside the vestry? Is the vestry their only outlet for ministry? Do they know their spiritual gifts, how they interact with others? Here's an exercise that can help accomplish this:

Spiritual gifts exercise

Consider giving each vestry member a spiritual gifts inventory and meeting with them personally to discuss what ministries they might be involved in that are compatible with their spiritual gifts. Does their ministry involvement match their spiritual gifts?

Or, there is a simpler exercise on page 81.

4. Missions and evangelism. Has each vestry member been involved at some level in reaching out beyond themselves for the sake of others? You might consider challenging them to go on a short-term mission trip or spend time working at a homeless shelter or volunteering to collect money for the Salvation Army. The exercise on page 82 can help highlight some of these issues.

***Closer Look**: Has each vestry member either been on a short-term mission trip or served in a local outreach ministry serving people beyond the membership of the church? Why not?*

The Leadership Level of Your Vestry

Leadership is influence. Effective vestries are not simply there to make decisions. They are responsible to discern God's direction for the church and to influence others in furtherance of the vision of the church. For the vestry to grow in their influence among the congregation, they must grow in their leadership level as well.

Refer to Chapter 3 ("Understanding Leadership"). Recall the five levels of leadership. If the leader does not raise the leadership level of those he is leading, he cannot rise to a higher level of leadership. True leaders raise the leadership level of followers. If the leadership ability of followers is not elevated, the purported leader is not really a leader. He or she may simply be a very talented individual.

Smaller churches can sustain themselves with very talented individuals. Larger churches need leaders to help them become more effective and mobilize more people.

The Commitment Level of Your Vestry

Members of the congregation not only look to the pastor for spiritual direction, they also look to the vestry to define the highest level of commitment in the congregation. The vestry must embody the vision of the church. Parishioners will usually use the commitment level of the vestry as a measure of their own commitment.

Personal Testimony Excercice.
Answer three questions:

What was my life like before I knew Jesus Christ as my Savior?

How did I come to accept Jesus Christ as my Savior?

What is life like for me since I accepted Jesus Christ as my Savior?

Spiritual Journey Exercise

Draw a timeline of your life. Divide the arrow into 10-year segments. With a colored pen, draw a line along that same timeline that shows major points in your life, consisting primarily of emotional or psychological highs and lows (this obviously is not a straight line). With a different colored pen, draw another line showing the spiritual highs and lows. Share this with one other person in the group.

Spiritual Gifts Exercise

Answer these questions:

What do I sing about? (What energizes me?)

What do I weep about? (What grieves me?)

What do I dream about? (What captures my attention?)

Spiritual Impact Exercise

Answer these questions:

Write down the names of the five most significant people in your life. How have they made an impact on your life?

Next, write down the names of five people on whom you've had an impact and why.

Church members notice when vestry members are present or absent for major parish events. The absence of several vestry members from key events in the life of the congregation tells parishioners that their attendance is not really important or necessary.

If the event is considered a major parish event, all vestry members should be present (unless their absence is for good cause). If attendance is effectively optional for vestry members, the event should not be considered a major parish event. The congregation will often reflect the commitment level of the vestry.

***Quick Insight**: Reflect on the past three major parish events. How many vestry members were present? How many absent? What does that tell you about the commitment level of your vestry?*

Vestry Elections

When seeking nominees for vestry membership, many churches will publish in their parish newsletter the following kind of announcement:

> Vestry elections will be held at the Annual Parish Meeting on Sunday, January 28, at 6:00 pm. The canons of the Episcopal Church provide three requirements for those wishing to serve on the vestry:
> 1. must be a confirmed member of the parish church;
> 2. must have been regular in attendance of Sunday Eucharists; and
> 3. must have been faithful in working, praying, and giving for the spread of the Kingdom of God.

What kind of vestry members will this church get? Probably your basic everyday church member. That may be fine for satisfying our needs for representative democracy, but it won't necessarily get any leaders nominated who have the oversight skills and management skills—in addition to spiritual maturity— necessary to serve on the vestry. Year after year, the United States Marines fill their recruitment quotas because they set the bar high. If you set your bar high, you'll get a much higher level vestry than if you only recruit based on the minimum requirements.

The quality of vestry members is only as good as the quality of candidates. Many vestry members get elected for the wrong reasons. Often, people who are elected are simply more well-known or well liked rather than rather than those who have the skills needed to serve on the vestry.

This is how the typical vestry member gets elected. Bill and Martha visit and eventually join the church. Soon, Bill gets asked to serve as usher. Bill loves ushering and is pretty good at it. After about a year, someone asks Bill to let his name be put forward for election to the vestry. Bill is honored; he hasn't really been a member of the church for very long but is pleased that he's recognized as "leadership material." So, Bill's name is placed on the ballot, and, lo and behold, Bill is elected. Amazing.

What account's for Bill's election to the vestry so soon after having joined the church? Because he's been a proven leader in the church? No. Because he's been in charge of a ministry and done a fine and trustworthy job? No. Because he's talked to lots of people about the vision and mission of the church and has some ideas of how to support the church in living into its vision? No.

Bill gets elected to the vestry because people see him week after week passing out the worship bulletins and he seems to be a pretty friendly and likable person. Bill is known and liked. He does a good job of passing out the worship bulletins each week. He's a friendly guy, gets along with lots of people. He's awfully well liked. The vestry could sure use someone like Bill. Why? (My apologies go to the ushers in the churches who also serve on their vestries. Many of them are fine vestry members.) The church in general, and the rector specifically, have no way of knowing the level of Bill's commitment to the church beyond a basic fulfillment of the canonical requirements as traditionally interpreted.

Does your church have any requirements for vestry membership beyond the stated canonical requirements? Are there certain skills needed among new vestry members for the church at this time? When you don't have any real requirements to serve beyond basic membership in the church, the church establishes the level of commitment and leadership at the lowest level rather than the highest level. A better way is to make the vestry a more exclusive organization, not in terms of being a part of the "in crowd" but in terms of being composed of those members that have exercised commitment and leadership at the highest levels and have the leadership and oversight skills necessary for effective service on a vestry.

Smaller churches often succumb to the temptation to fill the vestry with "warm bodies." Some churches will often nominate and elect people who are not very involved in the church in hopes that as they become more involved in the vestry, they will make a stronger commitment to the church. At other times churches will have vestries made up primarily of people new to the church. Many of these newcomers have no strong ties to the real people of influence and history in the church. Consequently, there develops a gap between the elected leadership of the church and many of the real powerbrokers of the church. When the vestry is composed mostly of newer members, the rector may believe that she has strong support for her agenda when in reality the long-standing influencers in the congregation feel marginalized and distanced from the rector. This is a recipe for conflict.

Chapter 9

Developing a Staff That Will Expand the Ministry

First who . . . then what.

Jim Collins, *Good to Great*

Almost every church has a staff. Not all staff members receive salaries; but all staff members, whether paid or volunteer, deserve to be managed well.

Initial Interview with the Staff

When the new pastor is called to serve the church, she should spend some time with the staff or the volunteers in charge of the major ministries of the church. Let them help you diagnose the organization. Ask these questions:

- What are the biggest challenges or obstacles the church is facing in the near future?

- What has caused these challenges?

- What things are we doing that we shouldn't be doing? Why are we doing them?

- What should we be doing that we are not doing? What do we need to accomplish those things?

- If you were me, what would you focus your attention on?

Asking the same people roughly the same questions will give you insight not only into the congregation but also into the congregational leaders themselves. Furthermore, listening carefully and eliciting their counsel, the new pastor comes first as a learner rather than the person with all the answers. You need not follow their advice, but you will have a much fuller picture of the church than you will have gotten from the parish profile.

When you first meet your staff, watch them during the day. Who is happy, and who is not? Do you know why? Notice the secretaries or receptionist. Secretaries and administrative assistants put a public face on your church. They are extensions of the ministry of the clergy and staff. A flat or unpleasant or even a frustrated response can do tremendous damage to the ministry of the church. If you notice these key people being fussy or unpleasant with people, they need to be told that their first responsibility is to smile and practice the gift of hospitality—or that they should consider that God might, in fact, be calling them to another line of work.

At our diocesan office, we playfully refer to our receptionist as "Diocesan Missioner for Hospitality." She does a wonderful job greeting people as they come in, recognizing people on the telephone by their voices, and truly putting people at ease. She understands that her job is to extend hospitality to all who encounter the diocesan office.

***Closer Look**: How does the staff interact with one another during the day? Do they laugh together? Talk about one another behind their back? Share prayer concerns?*

Working with Volunteer Staff

One of the challenges of working with volunteer leaders is that clergy often don't know how to manage them.

Ministry Position Descriptions

Provide volunteer staff with written position descriptions similar to those for paid staff. Even very small churches—which tend to convey instructions orally and informally—will benefit from written ministry descriptions, which tend to raise the level of expectation and therefore raise the level of quality. Further, one of the challenges that faces churches in the pastoral- to program–sized transition is the shift from an oral and informal way of relating to staff to a written, more programmatic approach. Providing written ministry descriptions in the smaller size church will also help transition the church to a more program-based approach to ministry and management.

Annual Salary of $1 per Year

The bishop of West Texas has expanded his staff with some creative funding. The diocese pays these key volunteers $1 per year. In addition, they receive an office, secretarial support, and continuing education assistance. They attend appropriate staff meetings and are involved in the budget-making process of the diocese. They are treated as full staff members for all intents and purposes—except their salary is only $1 per year. Because they receive a salary, they can also be released if they don't fulfill their responsibilities.

Motivating Your Staff

The two challenges that churches face in recruiting and retaining quality staff members are (1) churches historically pay less than the for-profit sector, and (2) as with most helping professions, there is rarely any real closure for tasks accomplished. Real estate agents close deals. Carpenters complete buildings. Attorneys finish cases and mark the files "closed." The work of church staff members is never done. How does a church motivate people in an increasingly consumer-oriented, accomplishment-motivated society?

Motivate Them with Mission

What is the mission of the church? People are not motivated by maintaining the status quo. Simply operating the denominational franchise fosters a maintenance mentality. Mission motivates. People find meaning in being a part of something larger than themselves. A church without a compelling mission will have an unmotivated staff.

Further, people need to be able to connect their area of responsibility to the larger mission. The more directly they see that their ministry connects to the larger mission of the church, the more motivated they will be. Help them to see that their ministry is an integral part of the mission of the church and how their ministry involvement is helping the church fulfill its vision.

Motivate Them with Goals

Don't ask people just to run a program. Staff members are motivated by goals that they participate in developing. Simply maintaining a program demotivates. Seeing growth encourages people to "go the second mile." Cost-of-living raises are sure-fire ways to reinforce a maintenance mentality. Simply giving a cost-of-living raise tells your staff, "You don't really have to do anything extra around here. We'll take care of you." If a staff member doesn't earn a merit increase, ask whether they are adding enough value to the organization to be retained.

Motivate Them with Feedback and Affirmation

People need to hear that they are doing a good job. They are also motivated by encouragement to do a better job; to know that someone is noticing. When someone has done well, praise them in front of their peers. In addition, it's not enough simply to affirm people publicly; match what you say about them publicly with what you say to them privately.

Motivate Them with Rewards (Yes, Rewards)

When you can, pay your staff well. Give merit increases as the church's income grows. Their good performance has contributed to the growth of the church. They should be rewarded accordingly. Even when the church's salaries are not as high as you would like, find ways to reward them. Give them a dinner and movie or a weekend away or a day off, or send them to a continuing education event (not in the same city where your church is located).

***Closer Look**: When was the last time you surprised your staff with something pleasant, like an afternoon off, a box of doughnuts, or Tootsie Roll pops in the afternoon?*

Motivate Them by Making Ministry Fun

Ministry should be fun. Proverbs 17:22 says, "A cheerful heart is good medicine." Check out the attitude around the church office. Do people joke with each other? Do they share stories about their home life? When people come into the office, do they feel welcomed, or do they get their business done and then leave? When staff members enjoy coming into the office, their attitude will draw others in as well. People's poor attitude and dour disposition will turn people away.

Thinking Through a Staff Meeting

Does your church have a staff meeting? Churches at every level should hold a regular staff meeting. If you have only one volunteer, you should still have a staff meeting. Even at the smaller size, a staff meeting will keep you focused on the ongoing life of your congregation, and it will also prepare you for greater responsibilities. As your church grows, it will become more complex; coordination becomes more of a challenge. A quality staff meeting can help move your church forward and keep everybody "reading off the same page."

Emphasis is on the word "quality." More than simply gathering the staff together, a quality staff meeting will do the following four things:

1. **Building community**: Recall the summary from the Henri Nouwen article, "Solitude to Community to Ministry." For church leaders to conduct the ministries of the church without building the staff into a community is like running a race with a 50-pound weight. The runner can move forward but not very fast and not very far. Prayer, sharing, and Bible study will help form the staff as a community of disciples.
2. **Exploring vision**: As the staff articulates and explores together the implications of the vision of the church, they learn also how to communicate the vision to the rest of the congregation. At times, the staff will serve as the sounding board for new initiatives and brainstorming. Their sharing and conversations will help them both to understand and to articulate more clearly the mission and vision of the church.
3. **Communicating information**: It is important that everyone know what's going on at the church. As the church grows in complexity, clear communication becomes more crucial. Staff members want to feel that they know what's going on.
4. **Creative thinking**: The energy that flows from a creative staff is tremendously stimulating for both the staff and the congregation. Mary Poppins tells the children that "a spoonful of sugar helps the medicine go down." Creativity turns maintenance into mission.

Planning the Staff Meeting

Using your staff meeting to help motivate your staff will require that you plan for each staff meeting ahead of time. Both the senior pastor as well as each staff member should come expecting to participate in the meeting. When no thought or planning is put into the meeting ahead of time, it communicates to the staff that the meeting isn't really important and that they don't really need to plan for their ministries either. If the agenda for your staff meeting is the same week after week, chances are your ministries will be the same week after week, and the staff will become increasingly unmotivated.

VHS: Vision, Huddle, Skill

Where are you leading the congregation? You must first lead your staff before you can lead the congregation. What do you want them to learn? Are there skills you want them to develop? Are there dynamics going on among the congregation that the staff needs to understand? Do you need to discuss certain talking points on certain subjects that you want everyone to be agreed on? Also, sharing ought to be an ongoing part of the staff gatherings—both personal sharing and caring for one another as well as the sharing of "resurrection stories" of the good things that God is doing in the life of the congregation.

Calendar

What's coming up? Going over the calendar keeps the staff from being surprised, from certain conflicts from developing, and allows the pastor to emphasize the importance of staff attendance and involvement.

Discussion and Brainstorming

Are there new policies that you want to introduce and implement? A new ministry starting that you want to introduce? Feedback on current ministry for improvement? Do you want to brainstorm certain ideas or plans?

Action Items

What needs to be done? Is there advertising that needs to occur for an upcoming event? Coordination among the staff for an event or a project? Does a new policy need to be explained or clarified?

Here's what a sample staff meeting agenda might look like:

VHS

Bible study: John 17 – Unity in the body of Christ

Information Items

1. Calendar items:
   - Convocational Meeting — October 9, 7:00 pm; St. Barnabas, Fredericksburg
   - Bishop's Visitation — October 12, both services
   - Alpha Retreat — Oct. 26–28; Wellspring Conference Center
   - Beginning of Discovery Class — Saturday, November 2, 9:00 am to noon
   - Rector's Appreciation Sunday — November 2
   - Joint Thanksgiving Service with St. Paul's Lutheran —Tuesday, Nov. 22; 7:30 pm
2. Diocesan Convention — Oct. 20–21; Episcopal School of Dallas
3. Newcomers to look out for – see handouts
4. Pastoral concerns in the parish

Discussion Items

1. Sunday services: How did it go? What was strong? Needs to be improved? How?
2. Newcomer's orientation: What are we doing? How can we improve?
3. Shrove Tuesday, Ash Wednesday, Holy Week, Easter: Brainstorm

Action Items

1. Coordination of Convocational Meeting
2. Staff and vestry dinner with bishop on Sunday, October 12
3. New health insurance coverage
4. Proposed newspaper articles or advertising

A Sample Ministry Plan

Businesses do it, but I've seen very few churches that do it. Higher performing churches do it. What is it? It is a business plan (or ministry plan). One of the best ways to build growth into the DNA of a church is to have each program staff member—even if there is only one program staff member, namely the pastor—put together a ministry plan.

What is a ministry plan? A ministry plan is a plan that the program staff member will implement during the coming year, along with the goals for each area. A ministry plan will keep one from being distracted from the important by the exigencies of the urgent. A ministry plan keeps one focused on the "big picture." A ministry plan will keep staff members accountable for accomplishing something positive by year's end rather than simply maintaining the ministries that are assigned.

Consider this scenario: A transitional or small program-sized church hires its first assistant priest. The congregation is excited at this addition and expects growth to result from the extra clerical assistance. After a while, conflicts may develop between the rector and the assistant; and the hoped-for growth does not materialize. Why not? The reason may be because the church did not hire another programmatic staff member to develop new programs and ministry. Rather, the church simply hired a helper for the rector to do more of those things that the rector simply doesn't have time for or just doesn't want to do. So, the assistant simply helps provide more pastoral oversight for the same number of people.

Or consider this situation: A church hires a youth pastor expecting the full-time person to grow the youth ministry. A year later, the same number of youth are involved in the youth ministry as the previous year. They are happier because they have more hands-on attention, but there aren't any more students involved. Why not? Because by not asking the new youth pastor to develop a ministry plan, we have encouraged this staff member simply to "run the program" rather than to develop the ministry. A ministry plan will both motivate and hold accountable the new staff member.

Here is a sample ministry plan.

YOUTH PASTOR

August 2001–July 2002

1. Youth Ministry Leadership and Oversight
   a. Provide supervision to the Junior High Ministry. Help establish Junior High Ministry goals.
   b. Enlist and develop youth sponsor (ministry teams) for both Junior High and Senior High. (Two teams for each ministry.)
   c. Implement and oversee parent education for Junior High and Senior High parents.
   d. Continue to develop and strengthen small-groups ministry for Junior High and Senior High.
   e. Develop and implement once-per-month combined worship for Junior High and Senior High along with every-week individual worship for Junior and Senior High, respectively.

2. High School Ministry Goals.
   a. Bring five new students into youth ministry through personal contacts.
   b. Five small-group leaders and apprentices (two Junior High and three High School groups).
   c. Sunday morning average of more than 50.
   d. Sunday evening average attendance of 60.
   e. Develop worship teams for both Junior High and Senior High Worship.
   f. 12 students on the Juarez mission trip.
   g. 12 students to Episcopal Youth Event.
   h. 15 students involved in local mission efforts.

Some Thoughts on Staff Development: Good to Great

In the book *Good to Great*, Jim Collins tells how he studied 1,435 good companies.[13] He examined their performance over 40 years and found the 11 companies that became great. Here's what he learned, along with some thoughts on staff development.

Get the Right People on Board First, Then Figure Out Their Strategy

So often churches—particularly smaller churches—hire people who are simply available. Because they are highly relational, they spend little time really formulating what they want a staff position to do and not much time looking for candidates and interviewing for the best person. Collins likens a business (church) to a bus. He says that companies that move from "good" to "great" start with "who" rather than "where." If you have the wrong people on the bus, it doesn't matter "where" you're going if those people can't get you there.

Face the Reality of the Situation, but Have Faith That You Can Prevail

Remember that Max DePree says that the first task of the leader is to define reality. A recent survey illustrates that reality and articulated reality don't always match. The Hartford Institute for Religious Research asked congregations to complete a survey that asked questions similar to those found on the parochial reports.[14] When the compilers of the survey compared the completed surveys with those of that congregation's parochial reports, it was apparent that the survey results often contradicted the parochial report data. Only those churches that were growing 10 percent or more per year "told the truth." The vast majority of churches—those stagnant or in decline—reported that they were doing better than their parochial reports indicated.

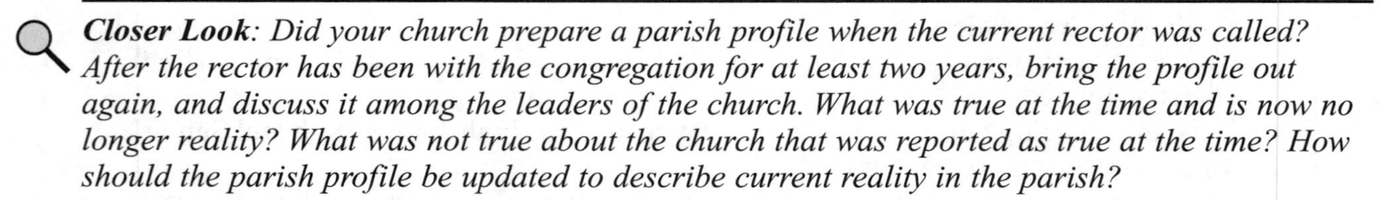

Closer Look*: Did your church prepare a parish profile when the current rector was called? After the rector has been with the congregation for at least two years, bring the profile out again, and discuss it among the leaders of the church. What was true at the time and is now no longer reality? What was not true about the church that was reported as true at the time? How should the parish profile be updated to describe current reality in the parish?*

It is important for the leader to "define reality," but it is equally important that the leader demonstrate faith in the forward progress of the congregation. I once read of a study of two test groups with individuals sticking their feet in a bucket of ice. Half the participants were by themselves and were told at the beginning to keep their feet in the ice as long as they could. The other half of those studied had other people in the room who encouraged them to keep their feet in the bucket of ice. They found that those who had people in the room encouraging them to keep their feet in the bucket of ice, on average, kept their feet in for twice as long. Encouragement can be very motivating.

Relentlessly Push Forward to Achieve Momentum

Don't "lurch back and forth." Leadership is hard work. Set personal and achievable goals. Announcing these goals and their achievement helps build momentum. What are the momentum indicators in your congregation?

Keep Your Focus on What Your Church Can Do Best

Some churches try to do too many things for their size. They model themselves after larger churches, thinking that they need to provide all the ministries and structure of larger churches. Because they don't have enough leaders for all the ministries they try to support, they end up doing several things poorly with many frustrated parishioners rather than a few things well. Peter Drucker, world-renowned management consultant, encourages both for-profit and non-profit organizations to ask, "Who is our customer, and what does the customer consider value?"

It's awfully difficult to move the congregation into a new direction of ministry—where growth often occurs—when the basic "goods and services" that are the staples of a congregation's life are not being carried out proficiently. What are the basic "goods and services" of your congregation? Start there and add quality to them before moving to more specialized ministries.

How Engaged Is Your Staff?

A recent study from the Gallup Organization of nearly 8,000 business units in 36 companies found a "positive and substantially meaningful" correlation between business success and highly engaged workers. Researchers developed 12 questions to mark the presence or absence of engagement. "If you satisfy their deep wants, employees become more engaged and will perform better," says James K. Harter, the senior research director.

Here are the 12 questions. How would your staff respond?

1. Do you know what is expected of you?

2. Do you have the materials you need to do your work right?

3. Do you have the chance to do what you do best every day?

4. In the last week, have you received recognition for doing good work?

5. Does your supervisor seem to care about you as a person?

6. Is there someone who encourages your development?

7. Does your opinion seem to count?

8. Does the mission/purpose statement of your company make you feel that your job is important?

9. Are your associates doing quality work?

10. Do you have a best friend at work?

11. In the last 6 months, has someone talked to you about your progress?

12. During the last year, have you had opportunities to learn and to grow?

And, here are some final questions for the senior pastor.

1. Are you staffed for maintenance or growth?

2. Are you staffed for yesterday or tomorrow?

3. Does your staff duplicate the ministry of the rector or expand it?

4. Is your staff expected to manage their programs or to expand them?

5. Do you have a regular staff meeting?

6. Does the church provide continuing education for staff?

7. Christmas bonuses? Merit raises?

Section 4
Using Administrative Changes to Effect Healthy Change

Chapter 10

Building Trust through Financial Accountability

To be trusted is a greater compliment than to be loved.

—George MacDonald

Stewardship is all about trust. God as Creator has entrusted the world and its resources to his creatures to be good stewards of those resources. God as the source of life has entrusted to us as individuals a variety of gifts and abilities in the living of our lives

Stewardship Is about Both Faithfulness and Perception

Only as we are faithful in the small things will God entrust us with the larger things. Only as the leaders of the church are faithful in their stewardship of the smaller resources will the congregation entrust those leaders with larger resources. People will only follow someone that they trust. Further, they will follow a person only as far as they can trust that person. The stewardship of church leadership is both about being faithful with the resources of the congregation (i.e., being trustworthy) as well as communicating that trustworthiness (i.e., the perception of being trustworthy).

Being trustworthy and being perceived as trustworthy are two different things. Sometimes the stewardship of individuals suffers, not because the leadership is not trustworthy, but because the leaders failed to communicate effectively those things that will help members of the congregation to see that the leadership is being faithful in its stewardship of the congregation's resources.

In Chapter 2, we talked about the importance of trust as a crucial element in the development of leadership. Only as the leader is trusted will those followers entrust the leader with risk in their lives. This is particularly true for the vestry and their fiduciary responsibility. It is not enough for the vestry to be faithful stewards of the resources of the congregation; they must also communicate that faithfulness in order to increase the trust of the congregation in their leaders.

The real work of the vestry is in the vision and mission of the church. Being faithful stewards as well as being perceived as faithful stewards of the finances of the church will then lead the congregation to entrust the vestry with leading them in vision and mission because they have been faithful with the finances of the congregation.

A Case Study

St. Francis', a fifty-year-old congregation, had been without a rector for more than two years when Father Michael was called to lead them. Before accepting that call, Father Michael looked into the parish finances and found several signs of trouble: the parish had no pledge drive even though their income was declining and they were operating on a dwindling budget; in the latest budget cuts—made just before his arrival—all operating funds for outreach had been removed; and (perhaps most tellingly) fully 25 percent of their budget was in designated funds and thus not entrusted to the control of the vestry.

The fact that many individual members designated their monetary contributions to their parish seemed to indicate to Father Michael that parishioners did not trust their vestry to make wise decisions about their money. He discovered that, about five years earlier, the community's highly regarded treasurer had embezzled from their endowment funds. Although the vestry and other church leaders apparently had moved diligently to protect their assets by reaching an agreement with the treasurer that ensured repayment of all missing funds, their proceedings had been done largely in secret—in a misplaced attempt to spare their disgraced former colleague further embarrassment and suffering. The upshot of this well-intentioned discretion was that their good work came across to the congregation looking like complicity and cover-up. For all intents and purposes, the congregation held their vestry directly responsible for the embezzlement!

Father Michael concluded that the financial trustworthiness of their vestry (either real or perceived) was *the* lively issue for this congregation. Before he would agree to accept their call, he made it a condition that the vestry conduct an audit of the church's finances to be completed by the first anniversary of his tenure.

When Did You Last Conduct a Financial Audit?

Conducting a financial audit for smaller churches need not be particularly expensive. There are various levels of audit, and yours may not require a professional CPA firm. Full-blown certified audits sometimes aren't necessary for smaller churches; an income expense review might be adequate instead.

***Closer Look**: Check your diocesan canons and talk to your diocesan administrator. You may discover alternative, less expensive ways of satisfying the audit requirements.*

Report the Results of the Audit

Report the results of the audit to the congregation. Because both trustworthiness and the perception of trustworthiness are important, it is important not only to conduct the audit, but to let the congregation know that the audit was, in fact, conducted. Report the initial recommendations of the auditor; later report on the changes made in response to the auditor's recommendations. Such in-depth reporting may not be necessary for a church where financial trust is not at issue, but it is necessary when there has been financial mismanagement in the past.

***Closer Look**: Ask a couple of parishioners if they recall when was the last time that the church conducted a financial audit. Were the results reported to the congregation? In any event, if it has been more than a year since the church conducted an audit, do it now.*

If the vestry balks at the expense of an audit, you might contact the bishop's office and have the bishop send a letter to the senior warden and the treasurer that an annual audit is required. Then have the canon to the ordinary or archdeacon follow up with a telephone call inquiring when the audit report will be completed.

Post the Vestry Minutes and Financial Reports

Post the minutes of monthly vestry meetings and the treasurer's report—both monthly and annually—on a bulletin board around the church. It is likely that hardly anyone will ever read these reports, but this communicates that the vestry leadership is being transparent in its financial dealings.

You may get the occasional "off the wall" question. Take the time to address these concerns individually and courteously. As you deal with each inquiry with transparency and integrity, word will spread throughout the church that there are no "dumb" questions nor secret dealings.

***Closer Look**: Are your treasurer's reports posted somewhere on the church premises so that the average concerned parishioner can check them out? Ask five parishioners at random if they can tell you where those reports are posted. Place a note in the parish newsletter: "**Did you know** that the monthly vestry minutes and treasurer's report are posted on the bulletin board in. . . ."*

Again, the importance here is both that the vestry be good stewards and that the congregation perceive that the vestry is trustworthy and transparent. If the congregation perceives that financial dealings are being done in secret and that they don't want anyone asking questions about the finances, the trust level will go down quickly—and deservedly so.

How Many Designated Funds Does the Church Have?

Another thing that the church did was to publish from time to time a summary of the various designated funds of the church. When there are a number of funding streams outside the operating fund of the church through various designated funds, there develops a sense that the finances of the church are done mysteriously, which leads parishioners to believe that the vestry does not welcome scrutiny of its financial dealings. The vestry may, in fact, attempt to be completely transparent in their financial dealings, but because of the complex nature of their funding, then the perception is that the vestry is doing things in secret. In addition, from time to time, place in the weekly worship bulletin an explanation of the purposes of these funds.

Another way to raise the awareness of the varied designated funds among the congregation is to place offering envelopes in the pews with a list of the various funds to which parishioners can contribute. This will not only bring new gifts into these funds, it will also communicate among the congregation that the vestry is being transparent in this area of its financial dealings.

***Quick Insight**: Quickly. How many designated funds does your church have? Does your typical highly committed member know that these funds exist? When did your church last report on the grants or expenditures of these funds?*

Learn to Understand the Treasurer's Report and Financial Statements

Sometimes, vestry members don't really understand the church's financial reports. They were elected and began serving on the vestry without any real orientation to the vestry. Although they have received the financial report month after month, it really seems to them like reading Greek. Then, in the frustration of their really wanting to understand the church's finances and the seemingly esoteric nature of them, these well-meaning and uninstructed vestry members become the greatest purveyors of distrust among the congregation.

The annual vestry orientation should include instructions on how to read the monthly treasurer's report, the church's balance sheet, the various funds belonging to the church, as well as the annual budget.

So much of trust is communicated by word of mouth. When one vestry member is asked about the church's finances who cannot explain them with ease, that uncertainty will be communicated to an average of 17 different people. However, as each vestry member becomes more knowledgeable about the church's financial condition and communicates positively with more people about that financial condition, the trust level of the congregation will increase significantly.

***Quick Insight**: What kinds of questions do members of your vestry ask during the financial report time? Does anyone ever relate the budget and expenditures to the vision and mission of the church?*

Using the Budget as a Teaching Tool

Which is a higher value for your church? Balancing the budget or doing mission? When the budget is presented to the congregation divorced from mission, people are more concerned about balancing the budget than what the budget is aiming to empower. I have heard of many churches asking parishioners to raise their pledge in order to have a balanced budget. This generally works only once. It is a short-term solution to a long-term problem.

The better question to be asked is: What does God want to do through the mission of St. Francis' Church, and how do the funds support that mission? It is important to connect the funding of the church with the vision of the church and with discrete examples of how that vision is being lived out and how the financial obedience of the congregation is providing those examples of ministry.

Budget descriptions should be graphically laden in order to catch the attention of parishioners. Often, when people are given only numbers, they look at those numbers as if they are deer with their eyes in the headlights. As their eyes glaze over at the vast array of numbers, they are tempted to look for small line items that they can ask questions about. These small line item questions are often a miniscule part of the overall budget and insignificant in the overall missional direction of the congregation, but these inquiries are well-meaning attempts by the questioners to exercise their fiduciary responsibilities on behalf of the church.

One way to teach the budget in a way that people can understand (This I learned from Bishop John MacNaughton.) is to ask the congregation if the church were to disappear, would anyone in the community notice? (This is the premise for the classic Jimmy Stewart movie *It's a Wonderful Life*.) Then, proceed to describe to the congregation how the community would be impaired because of all the ministries and people who would no longer be touching lives and making a difference in that community.

When dealing with budgetary presentation, ask the question: What message are we trying to communicate? Does our presentation communicate vision, expansion of ministry and mission, and God's faithfulness; or does it communicate maintenance, status quo, and fear?

Chapter 11

Building Credibility with Tangible Results by Improving Your Facilities

I love the house where you live, O LORD,
the place where your glory dwells.

Psalm 26:8

Looking at Your Church through Fresh Eyes

When my wife and I first saw the house that would become our first home together, we were excited. It was an older home, 60 years old at the time, with real character: columns on the front porch, French doors leading from the living room into the dining room and the den, and a breakfast room. The house was filled with the most wonderfully carved wooden antique furniture and gorgeous oriental rugs. It was a young couple's dream first home.

What a shock when the seller moved out and we moved in. The dear widow who had lived there for many years had kept the house closed and dark with heavy drapes covering the windows. When we first saw our dream house without the widow's furnishings and filled with glorious sunshine, we were stunned, shocked. Instead of a home with character, we saw only a house that looked old and tired. The walls had halos of smudge where furniture and pictures had been. We noticed pealing, chipping paint on all the woodwork. The wooden floors were two-toned, with the outlines of the widow's rugs clearly visible. Our hearts sank.

We saw our house from a fresh perspective. Our new perspective allowed us to see things that we had previously overlooked.

Churches are much the same. Visitors see things differently than do members. Because regular church members have grown comfortable with the church, they don't notice the things that visitors notice about your church.

***Quick Insight**: Walk through your parish hall or your office reception area. Do you see piles of clutter? Boxes stacked? Worn carpet? Visitors will notice these before you will.*

Our call to be good stewards of our facilities goes beyond material issues of preservation and safety. To be a good steward of one's church facilities is to be a good evangelist, because if we are to draw the unchurched into the fellowship of the church, we must give attention to the role that the condition of our facilities plays in terms of drawing them in or turning them away. The premise of this chapter is this: if the church cannot be trusted to take care of its physical facilities, how can they be entrusted with the care of people's souls?

As we have seen in Chapter 6 in the discussion about Maslow's hierarchy of needs, making physical improvements for the well-being and safety of the buildings are excellent ways for the new pastor to introduce change in a congregation. Improving the condition of church facilities that everyone can observe and appreciate will build credibility for deeper, intangible changes. Be careful not to spend too much money on these improvements, as you may not have earned that much trust. Instead, make improvements that are fairly visible and in higher traffic pattern areas but that don't cost so much as to lose credibility.

So, let's spend some time examining your church through three different perspectives: a visitor, a Most Attractive Church Award committee, and your camera. Each will reveal things about your church that you probably never noticed before and will help you target those improvements that will make your church a more warm and inviting place for people to hear the gospel and experience Christian community.

What Do Visitors See?

Walk with me on an imaginary tour of a church by a first-time visitor (we'll call her Sue) as we explore what she might encounter or the questions she might ask. Sue is a 32-year-old mom with two children, ages nine months and four years.

- As she drives by your church, will she even notice that it's there? Does it stand out from the surrounding buildings? Real estate agents call it "street view." What does your church look like from the street? Warm and inviting? Nondescript? What do newcomers or people who don't attend your church say? Have you heard people say, "I drive down that street all the time and have never noticed that there is a church there!"?

- Chances are that three or four blocks before your church she passed one of those "The Episcopal Church Welcomes You" signs. If you've already changed to one of the newer "We're Here for You," congratulations, you've probably already looked at your signs. If you haven't, drive by your "The Episcopal Church Welcomes You" sign, and look at it. What condition is it in? Do you see rust dribbling down the sign? Is the paint fresh or faded? Does it look fresh or tired? Can you easily find the church from five blocks away?

- While you're at it, drive around your neighborhood. Are there any main thoroughfares where a locater sign should be but isn't? Have you noticed the driving patterns around your church? Imagine that you don't know how to get to your church. Where would you place directional signs?

- Now, come back and drive past the church; don't pull in, yet. What about the church sign? Is your sign well lit? Does your nonlighted sign tell people that your church is only active during the daylight hours? Research indicates that 10 percent of your new members will come because of the church sign.

- Is your church sign perpendicular or parallel to the street? A sign parallel to the street is fine if you have people walking by the church—as was true in the 1940s. What size are the letters? What is the typical speed that cars drive on the street in front of your church, and can that typical driver read your church sign easily? Most people driving by don't have time to read a sign that is parallel to the street.

- Does it look fresh or is the paint peeling? Is the information accurate? Is the rector's or vicar's name in a paint color obviously fresher than the rest of the sign? (Does that convey a hidden message about your priest?)

- Suppose Sue drives by the church at a time when no one is around. What can she find out about the church? The name only? What time are the services? Some churches put out a Plexiglas magazine rack in the parking lot with church information similar to what you'll see in the front of houses for sale.

- Now, let's take a quick look at the building. What does she see? An attractive building and well-manicured lawn? Or unkept grass, growing weeds, unedged sidewalks? Flowers or weeds?

***Quick Insight**: If you were out looking to buy a church facility for your growing congregation, would you try to buy the church that you currently attend? Why or why not?*

- Where will Sue park? Do you have reserved parking for visitors or newcomers? Who gets the best parking places? The rector or vicar? The people who arrive earliest? You might consider having your staff and vestry park in the spots farthest away and save the best places for others. The least committed (newcomers) are often the ones who get the worst parking spaces because they don't arrive early enough. If they arrive 10 minutes after the start of the service and there is no parking space within a block, they probably will just keep on driving—and never become "newcomers!"

- By the way, how does your parking lot look? Is it clearly striped? Does it challenge the best shocks on a new car?

- Do Sue and her children know where to go? Is it obvious where the sanctuary is? Are the restrooms clearly marked? Are they clean? How will she find the nursery? What will be the condition of the nursery? Would you put your baby or grandbaby in that nursery? Are the toys old? Are there stuffed animals that breed germs? When were the toys last sanitized? How about the sheets in the cribs? Diapers? Wipes? Some churches instruct their childcare workers to change every baby's diaper 15 minutes before the worship service will end—even if the diaper doesn't need changing. This assures that the mother will get her baby back with a fresh diaper.

- What year does your nursery look like—2005 or 1955? Does it look bright and cheerful? Is the childcare worker friendly and welcoming? A couple with a small baby will return for a second visit if they are able to sit through the whole worship service without having to check on their child in the nursery. And they will return for a third visit if the childcare worker remembers the name of their child and welcomes her warmly.

- What about security for the babies? Is there a sign-in sheet? What will prevent someone unauthorized from gaining access to the children? Is your childcare worker licensed? Is she trained in CPR? If you have security measures in place, does Sue know this?

Closer Look: *Gather the mothers of infants and toddlers and would-be mothers in the church. Ask them to evaluate the nursery. What improvements would they make?*

- Sue finally gets to the worship service. How are the ushers: warm and friendly or "officious?" Do the ushers appear to be welcoming people to a celebration of the resurrection of Jesus Christ? Or do they act more like suspicious guards at an art museum? Do they proactively help to seat Sue or is their job finished once they've handed her the bulletin?

- Once Sue sits down, will she find it easy to follow the service? Or will she have to learn the "Episcopal shuffle:" pick up the bulletin, pick up the prayer book (what's that?), put down the prayer book, look up the hymn number, pick up the hymnal, put down the hymnal, look up the page number in the Book of Common Prayer, oops, no, we're in the Bible now. It's on the leaflet? I have four different leaflets. Oops, everyone's kneeling and I'm still standing. Oh, I'm so embarrassed. Now, I'm kneeling and everyone else is sitting.

- Does Sue get personally invited to the coffee hour? Where is it? Can it compete with Starbucks? Will anybody talk to her or will she stand there and watch people being real friendly to each other but not to her?

"Do not neglect to show hospitality to strangers, for by doing that some have entertained angels without knowing it" (Hebrews 13:2).

***Closer Look**: After completing this exercise as an imaginary visitor, invite a friend to your church, or someone from your child's soccer team, or go to the local Starbucks and hire a "temp" to visit your church and tell you what was attractive and appealing or distracting and repelling about their visit.*

The Most Attractive Church Award Committee

Imagine that your church has been nominated for the Most Attractive Church Award. The committee of three persons will come in one week to inspect your church. They will assign both positive points and negative points for what they see.

Now, imagine that you are inspecting the church in preparation for the visit by the committee. Walk outside the buildings and inside each building and through each room. Use the following chart to list the pluses and minuses of each area. What cleaning or repairs would you make that would qualify your church to win the Most Attractive Church Award?

Area:	
Pluses	Minuses
Cleaning or Repairs:	

Area:	
Pluses	Minuses
Cleaning or Repairs:	

Area:	
Pluses	Minuses
Cleaning or Repairs:	

Area:	
Pluses	Minuses
Cleaning or Repairs:	

Area:	
Pluses	Minuses
Cleaning or Repairs:	

Area:	
Pluses	Minuses
Cleaning or Repairs:	

Area:	
Pluses	Minuses
Cleaning or Repairs:	

Area:	
Pluses	Minuses
Cleaning or Repairs:	

Area:	
Pluses	Minuses
Cleaning or Repairs:	

Area:	
Pluses	Minuses
Cleaning or Repairs:	

Area:	
Pluses	Minuses
Cleaning or Repairs:	

Area:	
Pluses	Minuses
Cleaning or Repairs:	

Area:	
Pluses	Minuses
Cleaning or Repairs:	

Area:	
Pluses	Minuses
Cleaning or Repairs:	

Area:	
Pluses	Minuses
Cleaning or Repairs:	

Area:	
Pluses	Minuses
Cleaning or Repairs:	

Area:	
Pluses	Minuses
Cleaning or Repairs:	

Touring the Facilities through the Lens of Your Camera

When I was a child and heard my voice on a tape recorder for the first time, I didn't believe it was my voice. But if it was my voice, the tape recorder certainly distorted it. My friends assured me that my voice really did sound like that. Did you ever go back to visit your childhood neighborhood and become amazed at how small those houses are, and you thought that they were really large when you were a kid?

After you have completed the above two exercises, have someone take digital photographs of your church. Instruct this person to take pictures of every room, closet, window, narthex, parish hall—anything that catches her attention. This is another way of seeing the church through the eyes of the visitor.

Are there things that will cause embarrassment? Did you see things such as clutter or disrepair that you hadn't noticed before? Print out a preview sheet of slides and write notes next to each slide where clean-up, repairs, or improvements need to be made.

***Quick Insight**: Take a tour of your offices and classrooms. Without looking at your calendar, what year do the desks, chairs, and furniture tell you it is? Who gets the best equipment? What does that tell you about your church's values?*

How to Hold a Parish Work Day That Actually Gets a Lot Accomplished

Many churches hold clean-up, fix-up, paint-up work days. What typically happens is that the work day is announced for a certain Saturday at a certain time. Saturday comes, three men and two women show up. They sit drinking coffee for half an hour waiting for the others to show up. No one does. These faithful souls work for about 2 hours and then go home, vowing never to participate in a parish work day ever again.

Or, the church has a men's group that schedules their work day for a certain Saturday. Guys show up. They stand around, visit a while, the junior warden gives out assignments, and then different people plan trips to the local hardware store. Finally, about an hour later, the men finally get started, work 2 hours until it's time to go home and have lunch. They have spent a lot of time getting very little done. The day is long on fellowship and short on accomplishment. There must be a better way.

Actually, there is a better way. Here is how to hold a parish work day that actually gets a lot accomplished and is emotionally satisfying for all who participate:

This is what the parish work day looks like. Everyone gathers at 8 or 8:30 in the morning on that Saturday and receives their work assignments. Materials will be provided for them when they arrive. Coffee and soft drinks will be provided for a mid-morning break; lunch will be provided around noon. After lunch, crews are free to complete their work or leave as needed. These, then, are the steps:

First, have the junior warden or head of the buildings and grounds committee prepare a list of projects to be done, complete with materials needed.

Second, have this person recruit a person to serve as crew chief for each task or group of tasks. Provide each crew chief with the list of supplies that will be needed. They will have all the materials that will be needed to accomplish each project. Once you know how many crew chiefs you will have, purchase the materials for the work day and have them available for each crew chief.

Tell each crew chief that they are responsible to recruit their individual team members and bring their own tools for their particular assignments. Call the crew chiefs three days before the work day to see if they need any team members. Assign additional volunteers to work with the various teams and have the crew chief call each team member two days before the work day.

Third, recruit another crew chief to oversee the provision of coffee, soft drinks, and lunch. They will also have a cleaning project to do.

On the Sunday following the work day, announce at each worship service the results of the work accomplished and ask those who participated to stand for the applause and approval of the congregation.

Quick and Cheap Improvements

- Clean out flower beds and plant flowers.
- Add signs for parking for visitors and elderly people.
- Provide parking for handicapped.
- Provide flavored or specialty coffees for coffee hour (don't have a kitty for contributions).
- Repaint classrooms.
- Throw out old or cloth nursery toys and replace with new ones; restock nursery items.
- Place a bulletin board in the nursery with the church's childcare policy and photos of children.
- Add entrance ramps next to stairs leading into buildings.
- Remove parts of pews for wheelchairs in naves (but not on the first row).
- Build a free-standing kiosk on rollers for informational brochures about the church.
- Add an acrylic magazine holder for one-sheet flyers with information about church and place, along with sign, at an accessible, drive-by location in the parking lot..
- Place directional signs at various entry points around the church for newcomers.
- Trim shrubs, particularly around the outdoor sign.
- Repaint the outdoor sign if the name of the rector or vicar or service times have changed.
- Schedule a clutter tour. Walk through the various buildings of the church and identify and remove clutter

Churches deal with things unseen: people development, pastoral care, spiritual life. Growth in these areas is difficult to measure and can take years to realize. Further, improvements in pastoral care systems, quality of Sunday school or Christian education, and so on can take years for parishioners to recognize. However, physical improvements around the church are easily identifiable and can encourage members of the congregation that greater growth in the life of the church is on the way.

Chapter 12
Using the Annual Parish Meeting as an Opportunity for Motivation and Challenge

Public speaking is one of the best things I hate.

—Yogi Berra

Let's face it. How many of you really look forward to your annual parish meeting? There are typically three reactions from church members when they hear about the annual parish meeting. For the more politically motivated or institutionally supportive members, it is a time to elect new members to the vestry. For most others, it is a time of enduring all those boring reports and endless thank you's (unless you're one of those being thanked). For still others, it is a time to ask questions about the budget. Usually these questions are about minutiae in the budget, such as someone's pet ministry or a particular line item that caught their attention. The questions do not usually relate to how spending fulfills the church's mission or the general direction of the church—unless your congregation is in conflict, and we're not really going there in this book.

Under normal circumstances, the annual parish meeting is one of those maintenance things that has to be done because the canons require it. It's not very glamorous, hardly ever exciting, and usually greeted with all the enthusiasm of an ingrown toenail or cleaning out the lint trap of the clothes dryer.

What a lost opportunity most of our annual parish meetings are! We have an opportunity to speak to the primary leaders and influencers of the congregation, and instead of feeding them really nutritious vision we generally give them the pablum of maintenance. Instead of reading reports that no one really listens to, we should use this time to motivate the congregation to engage in mission, to build faith by celebrating the accomplishments during the previous year, and to challenge the church with the goals and opportunities that lie ahead.

What Are You Trying to Get Them to Do, Anyway?

For years I had a printed message taped to the surface of the pulpit where I preached Sunday after Sunday. It read, "What are you trying to get them to do, anyway?" That was a reminder to me that I wasn't preaching just to occupy 20 to 30 minutes. As the pastor of this flock, I was trying to motivate them to do something. This message prodded me always to have some sort of practical application or response among the congregation in my sermon.

When you think through your annual parish meeting, start with that same question, "What are you trying to get them to do, anyway?" Put yourself in your parishioners' pews. What do they need to hear that will add value to and make a difference in their lives as individuals? Where are you as the preacher trying to lead the church as a whole? The annual parish meeting is like the start of a race. This race will last all year. These runners will encounter obstacles, possible detours, relief stations, hills, and valleys all along the course. How are you going to prepare them for this year? How can you motivate them to "go the distance?"

The annual parish meeting ought to do two things: celebrate the successes and faithfulness of the congregation in the past year, and motivate and challenge the church with vision for the coming year. So, as you plan each part of the annual parish meeting ask, "Does this celebrate or motivate?"

Picking the Time

What is the best time to hold the annual parish meeting? Unless specified in your church's by-laws, the best time to hold the annual meeting is whenever you can get the most people present. For some this may be Sunday evening or a weekday evening with a parish meal. (If you do want to precede the meeting with a meal, don't do a potluck. For smaller churches, let the vestry members provide for the meal. If you are in a larger church, let the church's operating budget provide the meal.)

I have found the best time to get the most people to attend is on a Sunday morning. We have combined worship services and held the meeting for an hour to an hour and a half during the Sunday school time. Limiting the meeting to an hour lets people know that the business won't drag on too long. Having a time limit forces the planning to be done well and requires everyone to be short and to the point.

Presentation Media

Having a printed agenda and a handout summarizing all the pertinent statistics and summaries of the accomplishments during the past year will give the congregation a succinct message of the state of the parish. People don't like surprises, and they do like to know that the meeting has direction and purpose (as well as when it will end). In addition, have each program area list several accomplishments and one or two goals that it aims to accomplish. If you don't communicate the good things happening in the congregation, no one else will. This summary parish report can also be given to newcomers when they join the church. Be sure to use graphics to make the report interesting. Too much text makes the eyes glaze over.

The complete budget should be given to people who come, but there should also be a summary page with lots of clear charts as a part of the budget package. The budget needs to be translated for people to help them connect the dots between budget and ministry. Read one or two letters of appreciation the church has received from missionaries or recipients of assistance.

***Closer Look**: Look back at the printed materials from the last three annual parish meetings. What message do they send about the church? Is your church more text-oriented or graphics-oriented?*

When giving reports, use PowerPoint to make your presentations more interesting and memorable. We live in a highly visual culture. If you want to hold the attention of your parishioners under forty years of age, you must beg, borrow, or steal a projector and computer to assist in your presentation.

Imagine that the junior warden wants to schedule a major parish work day in the coming year. Instead of simply announcing this upcoming event at the annual parish meeting, she should make a PowerPoint presentation with digital photographs showing the work to be done. Show a nice part of the church and then an area to be repaired, or a nicely manicured flower garden and then the area of the church that needs more tender loving care. You'll find that such a graphic presentation will bring more people out for the work day.

Setting the Tone

The annual parish meeting is the family gathered; it's like a family reunion. During this time, people are catching up with each other, hearing the news, telling stories. The warmer you can make the time together the better. Begin the meeting by singing one of the great hymns of the faith or a renewal song that is a favorite of the congregation. It needs to be a "barn burner." The person leading the meeting should tell a joke or a humorous story at the beginning. Having people laugh loosens people up and provides a positive atmosphere.

Timing during the meeting should be crisp. Most churches will have a master of ceremonies or a verger to coordinate the liturgical assistants at a worship service. It is similarly helpful to have a master of ceremonies to cue the next speaker to be ready immediately after each presentation.

***Closer Look**: Review the attendance for the annual parish meeting for the last five years. Has the attendance increased or decreased? Would you attend your annual parish meeting if you didn't have to?*

The Rector's Address

As the captain of the ship, the rector sets the agenda for the church. The energy of the rector sends the primary message to the congregation as to how they should feel about their church. The rector's address at the annual parish meeting should celebrate the accomplishments of the past year, particularly the goals that had been articulated to the congregation the previous year;

express affection for the congregation and individuals within the congregation; challenge them to accomplish certain goals; and give the congregation a sense of the larger vision of what God is doing and wants to accomplish through the church. The address should be laced with humor and individual stories as well.

 ***Quick Insight**: If you are the rector or vicar, do you remember what you said at the last annual parish meeting? If you can't remember, why should anyone else?*

Holding Elections

When it comes to elections, the only thing that most people really care about is the results . . . so, keep things moving!

At the annual parish meeting, it is helpful to have the nominees stand and give their names so that people can identify them. If a nominee is unable to attend the annual parish meeting for a reason other than sudden illness, I would question whether they should be considered as a candidate for vestry. Service on the vestry represents the highest level of commitment in the parish. What message of commitment is sent when the nominee is absent for his or her own election?

Beyond the presentation of nominees for vestry position, the time between ballots can also be made more interesting and life-giving. We can learn a lesson from brain studies. Really.

Use the time between ballots—when votes are being counted—to do something completely different, something that will energize the congregation. An election is a very "left-brain" thing to do, according to medical studies that assign analytical, logical, rational, and objective activities to the left side of the human brain and more artistic, intuitive, random, and subjective activities to the right. If you use this time to give more reports—another left-brain activity—people will lose interest and tire out. Instead, alternate your left-brain activities with some right-brain activities: sing a congregational hymn or contemporary worship song that is a favorite, a real "war horse" (Why? Because if they have to work to sing, they are getting stuck back in the left-brain again!); engage in creative worship or prayer; lead the congregation in a litany of thanksgiving; have a parishioner share about how the church has been important in his or her life; give a PowerPoint presentation of photos of congregational life, a fun activity—as people look for themselves and their friends—that also reinforces the notion that the church is a community and not just an institution.

Section 5
Expanding Your Congregation's Reach

Chapter 13
Developing Worship That Helps People Engage the Presence of God

God is spirit, and his worshipers must worship in spirit and in truth.

John 4:24

"What's in Your Box?"

Do you remember when Coca-Cola scuttled the old formula and introduced the "new Coke" and it was such a disaster for the company? When Pepsi went head-to-head in blind taste tests, people generally preferred the taste of Pepsi to Coca-Cola. So, the folks at Coke reasoned that the taste was out of date and that if they simply changed the formula, that is, the taste, that even more people would buy their product.

Right? Wrong. People were upset. They didn't like the new flavor. It was too sweet, too, well, like Pepsi. It just wasn't Coke. So, what went wrong?

They went back to their marketing research firm and asked them that very question. The firm asked them this simple question, which they had asked before Coke changed their formula. The question was, "What's in your box?" That is, why do people buy Coke? Or, translated another way, what is Coke all about?

They had asked this question before and determined that it was the taste that was in the box. They simply had a great product, and if they made their great product even better, then even more people would buy more Coca-Cola. Obviously, they had missed something. They reflected on that question and finally decided that Coca-Cola was an American institution and that it was the unchanging nature that was in their box. They reasoned that when they changed the formula, they changed all that Coke stood for, namely, Coke as an American institution. So, they reintroduced Coke Classic as the centerpiece of their product line, and now you'll find slogans like "Always Coke" as part of their marketing plan.

Let's ask the same question of the Episcopal Church. What's in our box? The answer that we most often get is: liturgy is in our box. We have a wonderful liturgy.

True, the Episcopal Church has a wonderful liturgy. The language and the ceremonies give the worshiper a sense of the holy. Rooted in history with both contemporary and traditional language choices, the liturgy connects the worshiper with the historical expression of the Christian community through the ages. However, if having a rich and deeply spiritual liturgy were all that people are looking for, we would not have lost more than a million members since 1965. Could it be that people want more than great liturgy?

The Challenge of Casualness

In the United States, we live in a culture that has become increasingly more casual. There was a time when both men and women wore hats and women wore gloves in public. No one would dare wear a baseball cap in a restaurant. If you look at pictures of major league baseball games from years gone by, you will see the men in those pictures wearing suits and ties and hats to the ballpark. Even in our own Episcopal Church, we have seen the relaxation of dress standards. Women no longer wear mantillas (lacy prayer shawls) or even hats to church. Visit any Episcopal Church and you'll find people dressed in everything from ties to shorts, polished leather shoes to tennis shoes.

So, we have to ask the question: how can the church engage people who seem to prefer increasing casualness in their daily life with a liturgy that remains more formal?

Actually, there's another challenge that we have to address that is really a corollary to the challenge of our formality. Loren Meade has articulated this concern for us.

The Challenge of a Cool Spirituality

The typical formality of our liturgy has produced what Loren Meade of the Alban Institute calls a "cool spirituality." Here is Meade's description of what he means by "cool spirituality:"

It had a depth and power that helped people through enormous trials and carried them through long hard journeys that tested them in every way. . . . What I learned about . . . growing into God was surrounded by "oughts:" how one ought to pray, how one cleansed oneself for communion with God. The way to God was a long, difficult road that I learned about. It was a road with many detours—on which I seemed to be most of the time. There was not a lot of joy associated with the walk.[15]

His response to this critique is to challenge the Episcopal Church to incorporate a more charismatic expression into its worship life: "I propose that the third challenge the churches must meet to build a church for the future is to find ways to bring this charismatic experience of spirituality into the heart of the Christian experience and bind it fully into the very structures and systems of the religious world of the churches."[16] He compares and contrasts the traditional expressions of spirituality with the more charismatic spirituality. When the traditional form of spirituality decays, Meade says, it becomes "a stuffy, dry, lifeless formality. Many members of the traditional churches have lived in such a straitjacket of their tradition that they have never found the power available in that very tradition—consequently their lives quietly go rigid and dry."[17] Younger generations, he says, "unwilling to pack their emotions in dry ice, simply opt . . . for other venues in which to find vitality."[18] He then compares a decaying traditional spirituality with a decaying charismatic spirituality. "When charismatic spirituality decays, it goes in another direction. As in the case of traditional spirituality, it becomes a parody of its strengths. Charismatic spirituality at its worst degenerates into spiritual pride."[19]

Meade says that our usual way of managing such differences is to choose one form over the other, to embrace one spirituality and eliminate the other. He suggests that the necessary solution is to view these "polar opposites" not as exclusive categories in which the church chooses one expression of spirituality and denigrates the other but rather to find creative ways for them to coexist within the churches.[20] Citing the work of Barry Johnson, Meade says that polar opposites actually need each other to maintain health. When each form of spirituality begins to decay, the more its worst characteristics come to the forefront. The health of the church is thus enhanced by the vitality of each of these expressions of spirituality.[21] Meade is calling essentially for the "warming up" of the spirituality temperature in Episcopal worship and the fostering of greater intimacy among the worshipers.

***Closer Look**: Reflect on the last three worship services. Do you recall the vibrancy of the liturgical responses? What kind of response were people expected to make? Or were they? How was the hymn singing?*

So, is the Episcopal liturgy an anachronistic relic of days gone by that needs to be radically reformed? I believe not. I believe that "these bones can live." The largest Episcopal Church in the country has an average Sunday attendance of 2,200. Although that seems to pale in comparison with some of the larger megachurches that average more than 15,000 per weekend, the fact that an average of more than 2,000 people attend an Episcopal Church with an Episcopal liturgy indicates that the liturgy is not what has caused our denomination to be in decline.

Before we get to specific recommendations of how to do that, we need to do some theology and cultural observation.

Mysterium Tremendum et Fascinens and the Ford Mustang

We read in Chapter 7 about the importance of mental models. We said that a mental model represents a psychological representation that the mind uses to understand real and hypothetical situations. A mental model is a sort of small-scale reality that allows people to anticipate events in order to give guidance for planning or simply for understanding. So, when it comes to planning liturgy, I'd like to suggest two mental models: Mysterium Tremendum et Fascinens and the Ford Mustang.

First, Mysterium Tremendum et Fascinens: this phrase comes from Rudolph Otto's *The Idea of the Holy*.[22] Otto says that as human beings, we have a need for the numinous. We are drawn to the Holy. However, when humans encounter the Holy, two different movements take place between the created and the Creator. Otto describes the fear and awe of God as the sense of mysterium tremendum. When we sense God's presence, we are made aware of His "overpoweringness" and

His majesty. We are so small and God is so large that we shrink in fear. God is pure holiness, and we are not. As my church history professor used to say, "One does not get chummy with the Almighty."

Yet, we are also allured by the presence of God. In the fascinens of our response to the Holy, we find that there is something fascinating, full of energy, and "uniquely attractive" and compelling about God that draws us to Him even as we are "quaking in our boots." This is the sense of which St. Augustine writes when he says that "our souls are restless until they find their rest in Thee, O Lord."

So, we are repelled by and drawn to the presence of God, both at the same time. Our encounter of the Holy is a continual and ongoing contradiction.

A cool spirituality reinforces only the mysterium tremendum aspect of our encounter with God. To have a holistic experience of worship, we must also incorporate elements of fascinens.

We see this contrapuntal, "repelling-alluring" movement expressed in contemporary American culture. Consider the redesign of the Ford Mustang.

In the mid-1960s, Ford Motor Company introduced the Ford Mustang. It was sleek, had beautiful lines, and to own one was every teenage boy's dream. After several years, the lines on the Mustang became less and less distinctive. As the Ford Mustang's design became less like the original and turned into more of a small inexpensive car, it came to look like just any old car. Consequently, sales declined. Then, in the 1990s, the Ford Mustang returned to its original design, with its sporty lines, slightly elevated hood, and fake air scoops on the sides. But, it didn't simply return to the original design; they improved upon it. They adopted the former sporty design but added the newer improvements. Sales increased again.

Others saw this trend and followed suit. McDonald's brought back its golden arches and red roof design, but they added the accessibility feature of being able to refill your soft drink from the dispenser in the dining area without having to ask the cashier. The Volkswagen Beetle was brought back to America after a 22-year hiatus but with the trunk in the back and better air conditioning.

The resurgence of the Celtic tradition has also tapped into this longing for historical connectedness. One of the newer singing groups that is growing in popularity is called "Mediaeval Babes." They have taken texts and tunes from the Middle Ages and contemporized them to make them more accessible to modern (postmodern?) tastes.

***Quick Insight**: Have you noticed the number of reunion services, dating services, and Internet chat rooms that have grown in the American culture? What does this say about the hunger for community?*

What this tells us is that there is a yearning in the American psyche for rootedness but accessibility. People aren't altogether at home in this new millennium. One detects in the popular culture that people are longing for ancient ways, ancient connectedness—even if "ancient" only goes back 40 years at times. But, they also want access to that ancientness than we have not been adequately providing. It's like the Ford Mustang: they want those classic lines, but they also like the modern improvements that make it an even better automobile. People are yearning for the experience of both mysterium tremendum as well as fascinens when we encounter the Holy.

Robert Webber, the Myers Professor of Ministry at Northern Seminary, has captured this phenomenon with his phrase, "ancient-future."[23] We also see this being expressed in the American church through the "emerging church" movement, which blends elements of traditional, ancient liturgies but repackages them in ways that make those liturgies more accessible to younger generations. Two recent books describe this phenomenon as "Vintage Christianity for New Generations."[24]

As a denomination, we have tradition and formality down pretty well. The next step is to infuse our more formal worship services with both energy, and intimacy and accessibility that will supply the warmer spirituality, the sense of fascinens, the future-oriented worship that the American soul is looking for.

Now, let's add what we've learned to our liturgy.

Making Liturgy Accessible

The Episcopal Church in general and local congregations individually must find ways to make liturgy more accessible and, thus, more participatory while retaining its historical underpinnings. Here are some recommendations that could easily be adopted.

Fully Printed Service Leaflet of the Liturgy

Consider printing the texts of the liturgy and music or lyrics in toto for each worship service. It is awkward for the newcomer to flip between worship leaflet, pages in the prayer book, and scripture leaflets or pew Bibles.

I recently sat down with my prayer book, hymnal, worship leaflet, and scripture insert and counted the number of times I had to change from the prayer book to the hymnal to the worship leaflet, to the collect or scripture reading for a typical Rite 2 service of Holy Eucharist. My hands had to change book or leaflet 33 times! Add to this whether to stand, kneel, or sit, and one can imagine the average newcomer must be totally confused and intimidated.

Kevin Martin, director of Vital Church Ministries and former Canon for Congregational Development in the Diocese of Texas, says that he knows of no growing church with an average Sunday attendance of 400 or more that does not print in full the liturgy in its worship leaflet.

Instructed Eucharist

A great way to help worshipers understand and appreciate the liturgy is to conduct an instructed Eucharist from time to time on Sunday morning. It can be a really powerful experience for the priest or deacon to describe their love for the liturgy and then to allow the congregation to share in that experience. Some might object that a running commentary would "destroy the beauty of the Eucharist." Actually, such an attitude strikes me as Gnosticism and elitism: "If people can't understand it on their own, well, maybe they don't need to understand it at all."

Worship Bulletin Blurbs

Have you noticed how CNN, CNBC and Fox News will run a headline news ticker at the bottom of their television broadcast? They understand that people are able to multitask and often want to know more than what is being said.

Our liturgy has so many gems that we can greatly enhance worshipers' experience and understanding of the liturgy by printing informational blurbs, or marginal notes, concerning different aspects of the liturgy in the worship bulletin. For example, did you know that the "Collect for Purity" was written by John Chrysostom, which means, John Golden-mouth, for his eloquence in speaking? Or that Eucharistic Prayer D is the oldest liturgy in continual use by the church and is authorized by the Episcopal, Roman Catholic, and Orthodox churches? Or, why do people make the sign of the cross, or three signs of the cross at the reading of the Gospel, why is it called a "Sequence," particularly when it used to be called the "Gradual," and so on? Providing this kind of information to worshipers will deepen their understanding of our rich liturgical heritage and enhance their worship experience.

"Extemporaneous" Teaching Moments

Another way to make liturgical worship more understandable and which would enhance the newcomer's experience of liturgical worship is to have planned "extemporaneous" explanations of the significance of different portions of the liturgy. At a minimum, the celebrant should at every service give an explicit invitation to Holy Communion as well as instructions concerning how to receive communion. In addition, include instructions that allow newcomers to come forward to receive a blessing without receiving communion if they are not baptized or not in a place where they can receive communion without feeling embarrassed.

Why is "extemporaneous" in quotes? Because, to be effective, they should not really be extemporaneous; rather, they should be delivered in an extemporaneous manner. The leader should write out these comments and practice them so that they come across as natural commentary to the liturgy, not as reading the rubrics to the congregation. These "ad libbed" additions to the liturgy need to be succinct, to the point, and informative. So, you want to pack in as much information in as few words as possible. These are, after all, additions to the liturgy. They are intended to enhance the liturgical experience, not to replace or overshadow the liturgy.

One parenthetical note about announcements: write these out beforehand and practice saying them so that on Sunday morning they sound natural but don't go on for too long. In my experience, generally the larger the church, the shorter the announcements.

Liturgical Leadership

Charles Bartow, professor of speech and homiletics, has written an excellent book for those who lead worship: *Effective Speech Communication in Leading Worship*.[25] Bartow makes the point several times in his book that the worship leader, preacher, and the reader of Scripture must all be personally engaged in worship and with the worshippers in the congregation. He continuously calls for the worship leader to make eye contact with the worship participants, for the reader to read with emphasis and inflection, and for the preacher to speak clearly and confidently.

For example, Bartow gives three principles for the person leading the congregation in the confession of sin and absolution in order to turn this part of the liturgical rite from rote, sometimes mumbling and disengaged recitation to a life-giving, truly common confession. First, the invitation to confession should be spoken directly to the people, eye to eye, and it should sound like an invitation and not a warning. Also, the confession itself should be led in a clear, strong voice that helps the congregation to pray as one with expectancy, hope, and trust. Finally, the absolution should be confident and forthright, not guarded and tentative.[26] In similar manner, the Eucharistic prayer should be spoken with direct eye focus on the congregation, and the words should be spoken so that the congregation actually has something to which it can respond.[27]

***Quick Insight**: Next Sunday, listen to the congregational responses. Are they full of energy, pedantic, mumbling, noncommittal? Congregational responses are often reflective of liturgical leadership.*

Have you ever been in a worship service and heard really lethargic liturgical responses? Next time you notice the congregation giving an uninspiring response, without chiding them, have the congregation repeat the appropriate response with the energy and vitality that the liturgy deserves.

Making Music Accessible

In his book, *44 Ways to Increase Church Attendance*, Lyle Schaller writes a full chapter entitled "Begin with the Worship Experience."[28] Schaller says that to increase church attendance, the leader must begin with the worship experience. However, he places his advice to evaluate the music at the end of this chapter. His reason for placing his recommendations about music at the end, he wryly notes, is "to provide the cowards with a less dangerous course of action."[29] Yet, for the church wanting to make worship accessible, music is really the starting place.

Many have said that if our church would simply add contemporary music, that we would bring back the young people. However, "contemporary music" in a religious setting can have two completely opposite meanings. It can mean difficult atonal mass settings by avant garde classical composers or it can mean a sort of soft rock "praise music" of a very specific kind.

Who Is Your Target Population?

Remember the Peter Drucker question: who is our customer? Who is our target population? Who are we aiming to reach? The issue with respect to music is not: what do I as the musician like? Instead, ask the question: what kind of music will help people who are our target audience to engage the presence of God? Some people simply don't like contemporary styles of music. Other people don't like hymns. Many people like certain hymns but don't really like more modern atonal arrangements to hymns.

The core value to be affirmed is to be culturally connected to our target population. The church is a missionary community that must engage the culture at the culture's starting point. Thus, we begin with the hearer and ask how we can best communicate with this certain type of hearer. Music is not a unilateral act. It is participatory in nature. Music that is inaccessible to the worshipper fails to allow the worshipper to participate in worship.

An individual congregation might choose to limit its musical expressions to classical music and hymn singing, but if there are no other Episcopal churches in the area that offer alternative musical style offerings, then a large portion of the surrounding population may, in fact, be missed. Or, a church might offer multiple services, aimed at reaching different constituencies. One size does not fit all.

Style of Music Deemed Appropriate

Not only should music be culturally connected to the target population, it should also be culturally connected to the institutional culture. The kind of music that a person enjoys listening to or singing for pleasure may not be the kind of music that that person believes is appropriate for worship. Although I may enjoy listening to Willie Nelson sing "Will the Circle Be Unbroken," I may not have a sense of fulfilling worship by having sung that song on Sunday morning.

***Quick Insight**: Next Sunday, sit back and listen to the congregational singing. Which hymns does the congregation participate in? Do they sing the responses or leave the service music to the choir? When people leave church, do they have smiles on their faces or are they somber?*

Can We as a Congregation Do This Music Well?

A third concern for the local congregation is: can we as a congregation do this music well? Some hymnody is simply too difficult for the average person to sing. The musical arrangement of some hymns may be too difficult for an individual organist or keyboardist to play. When a priest friend of mine first arrived at a new parish in New York City in the 1980s, she reported that the only hymn the congregation sang really well was, "All Hail the Power of Jesus' Name." Rather than have the congregation sing a variety of hymns poorly, this smart priest had them sing "All Hail the Power of Jesus' Name" every Sunday. Instead of becoming boring to the congregation, they sang it with increasing gusto each Sunday, until the hymn attained something like "theme song" status among them. The Promise Keepers movement has been tremendously successful in getting men to sing hymns. The hymns that they sing are pitched several keys lower than found in standard hymnals, and the arrangements are more contemporary in their orchestration.

Familiarity

A fourth factor for consideration when planning music for congregational singing is familiarity. How often do you introduce music, and how often do people get to sing hymns or songs that are particularly beloved by the congregation? If you will reduce the number of hymns and repeat the singing of certain hymns that are special to your congregation, people will be able to sing more vibrantly, and worship will be much more satisfying. A good rule of thumb is always to end the service with a "war horse"—a tried and true hymn or song. You want to give people a song or hymn that they will hum as they leave. Most churches sing too many hymns and as a result reduce the congregational participation.

Making Preaching Accessible

The typical sermon in the typical Episcopal Church today is the lecture-style sermon. The preacher who wishes to catch the attention of listeners in this media-soaked age, where the typical attention span is subconsciously trained by the length of time between commercials—approximately 7 minutes—faces a tremendously daunting task. Yet, if the church is to reach out to this generation of communication-rich patrons, its bearers of the Word of God must find ways to do so effectively.

***Quick Insight**: If you think you're a good preacher, ask yourself how often parishioners ask you for copies of your sermons. Because preachers often hear themselves only and not other preachers, they often don't have a good measure of their true effectiveness.*

Three Kinds of Learners

The average pew holds a wide range of people who process information differently. People learn in a variety of styles. Most people will have one predominant style of learning. Knowing that there are different kinds of learners and responding to them accordingly will allow the preacher to engage more people.

Learning styles fall into three basic groups: auditory, visual, and kinesthetic.[30] Auditory learners—or listeners—prefer to listen to books on tape rather than to read them. The auditory listener will respond to stories that touch the imagination. They want the speaker to "paint a picture with words." Instead of telling a story about sitting around a cabin in the winter, describe the rustic setting of the cabin, the smell of the fire in the fireplace, the aroma of freshly brewed coffee, and the still crisp chill in the air that hasn't been replaced by the warmth of the fire.

Next, some people in the congregation will be visual learners, or watchers. If an auditory learner prefers to learn how to get from point A to point B by hearing step-by-step instructions, a visual learner wants to see a map. In church, the colors of the procession or the artwork in the sanctuary speak to them—saying more, sometimes, than the appointed lessons. The expressions on the faces of choir members means as much to a visual learner as the music being sung. Visual learners need "visual aids" in order to be drawn into the sermon. For example, in order to engage the visual learner in a story about a baseball player, the preacher might actually step away from the pulpit and pantomime the motions of the batter. Another way to engage the visual learner is to print a simple bullet outline of the day's sermon in the service bulletin.

The third kind of learner is the kinesthetic learner, or mover. The kinesthetic learner wants to be actively and physically involved in the service. The preacher engages the kinesthetic learner by allowing this kind of learner to have a sense of participation in the sermon. It is helpful for the preacher to engage the kinesthetic learner in some sort of physical way. If a drama is used for a setup or illustration for the sermon, the kinesthetic learner will learn better by some sort of active participation. The "worship aerobics" of frequent standing and kneeling so common in many Episcopal churches are particularly meaningful to kinesthetic learners. Laughter (when it is an appropriate reaction to a colorful story told by the preacher) is another favorite way for kinesthetic learners to get actively involved in the worship.

Preachers constantly miss opportunities to engage the congregation physically. In a sermon about the woman who was healed by touching the hem of Jesus' garment, the preacher might ask each person to take another person's hand and meditate for several moments on the power of touch. Or the preacher might ask everyone to turn in his or her seat and meditate for several moments on a Bible scene depicted in one of the sanctuary's stained glass windows (an exercise that also will excite the interest of visual learners).

Murray Frick proposes six styles of sermons that allow the preacher to engage different styles of learners in different ways.[31] For those who think that presenting different styles of sermons is new or improper or "dumbing down" to the people in the pew, he directs the preacher to "the classic book on communication—the Bible. . . . Jesus himself used a variety of learning experiences to teach people around him. He drew in the sand, pointed to a withered tree, held up a coin, welcomed children to his side, and washed his disciples' feet."[32] The Bible is full of all forms of communication: dramatic storytelling, dialogue, letters, object lessons, and emotionally powerful stories. To engage this generation of learners who learn in a variety of ways, each sermon must connect with the hearers, the watchers, and the touchers.

The Difference between Pastoral Preaching and Leadership Preaching

The question we dealt with earlier was, "What are you trying to get them to do, anyway?" Isn't that the ultimate question for every preacher?

Not only does the preacher have the responsibility to be the pastor to individuals, the preacher also has the responsibility to pastor the congregation. I am calling the former, "pastoral preaching" and the latter "leadership preaching." Most preachers provide good pastoral care from the pulpit. But the preacher must provide leadership of the congregation from the pulpit as well. Both kinds of preaching are necessary for the health of the congregation into the future.

Let's explore the differences between pastoring individuals and leading the congregation from the pulpit.

1. Pastoral versus visionary. In pastoral preaching, the emphasis is on caring and nurturing. In leadership preaching, the preacher presses toward vision, direction, and progress toward a preferred future—in alignment with the vision of the church. In the Diocese of West Texas, the bishop has the newly installed rector preach at his or her own installation as rector. He asks that the new rector preach on the vision for the congregation. What an excellent way for the rector and congregation at this formative time to engage in the future—as well as the past—of the congregation.

Vison, however, must be repeated. To communicate the vision, the preacher should articulate the church's vision and illustrate it with stories from the life of the congregation on a regular basis. So often we seem to think that once we have spoken the vision "they" ought to get it, so now let's move on to something else. (Hint: "They" often don't get it. "They" often think, "this, too, shall pass.")

2. Individual application versus whole body application. Pastoral preaching to individuals centers on how can I apply this text to my life. Leadership preaching to the congregation involves how the text is applied to the general life and direction of the congregation: how can I apply this to my life as opposed to where are we headed as a congregation?

3. Present orientation versus future orientation. Pastoral preaching aims at connecting the hearer to his or her world today. Leadership preaching places its message into the future, calling people to stretch and exercise their faith for the preferred future.

4. Read the atmosphere versus shape the atmosphere. By atmosphere, I mean the overall climate; attitude of the church. A good pastoral care giver is sensitive to "what's going on" in the congregation. However, one who leads the congregation from the pulpit does the same but goes the second mile with an intentional effort to sustain morale or shift it in a more positive direction or build on the existing momentum.

5. Measure by personal transformation versus measure by personal transformation and organizational progress. Effective preaching is measured by how lives are changed and disciples strengthened. Leadership preaching does the same but includes how the congregation as a whole is transformed and how individuals participate in that corporate transformation.

A few other points:

1. As rector, vicar, and/or staff, have you established goals for the coming year that you can address in your sermons? This provides continuity between the vision, living into the mission of the church, and your role in leading through preaching.

2. Do you plan your sermon themes out by the year? Preaching in series and planning your topics a year at a time allows this same continuity between vision and mission.

3. You may have to preach from a text not in the lectionary for that Sunday. Gasp! My liturgics professor would have my head. Although the lectionary is a wonderful road map for the liturgical year, sometimes sermons need to be preached that fall outside the regular course of lectionary readings. Sometimes it is equally amazing how the scriptures appointed for that Sunday will speak precisely on point of what the congregation needs to hear at that time.

4. Consider posting the titles of the sermons in your series. This gives people something to look forward to and a reason to invite their friends.

Chapter 14

Reaching Beyond Your Church by Raising Your Church's Profile in the Community

I will give you as a light to the nations,
that my salvation may reach
to the end of the earth.

—Isaiah 49:6

We live in a post-Christendom culture where the church no longer has "home field advantage." Christendom is the understanding that the church and culture and cultural institutions reinforce each other. In the 1950s, church attendance was considered de rigueur. The popular culture and public institutions reinforced the values of the church. Public schools led their students in praying the Lord's Prayer. There was prayer before assemblies and prayer before sporting events.

At the beginning of the third millennium, we find that many Americans are attracted to spirituality . . . but not necessarily to Christianity; sometimes, people are intentional Christians but do not participate in church.

"If you build it, they will come" certainly worked in the movie *Field of Dreams*, and it worked quite well for the Episcopal Church and other mainline denominations in the 1950s. No longer. We are a church with beautiful architecture, rich historic liturgy, and a deep appreciation for sacred music. However, as a denomination, we are now smaller than we were in 1950. Meanwhile, the U.S. population since 1950 has nearly doubled.

One of the things that we can do as a church is to be more intentionally visible in our communities. In the 1950s, denominational affiliation meant more to people than it does today; we no longer live in a culture in which most seekers are willing to look for and locate the nearest Episcopal (or Methodist or Presbyterian) church. Those little "The Episcopal Church Welcomes You—Five Blocks" signs just aren't enough anymore. So, here are some suggestions for increasing your church's visibility.

The Pastor as the Number One Ambassador to the Community

It all starts with the pastor. The rector or vicar can do an awful lot to bring people to the church through her involvement in the community. She should see herself as the number one ambassador for the church to the community.

There are a variety of ways for the pastor to be involved in the community. Of course, she must balance the needs of her congregation with her level of involvement. Also, the profile of the pastor will vary with the size of the community. The smaller the community, the easier it is to have a higher profile. Also, the smaller the community, the more the absence of the pastor's community involvement is noticed in the community at large. Here are just a few examples:

- Join a service organization—a must in a smaller community.
- Attend high school sporting events—in a Texas small town, going to the high school football game should be a part of the position description. In your area, it may be basketball, or hockey, or whatever. Be seen.
- Serve on local boards—such as Hospice, Habitat for Humanity, social services, and so on.
- Assist with community disaster-relief efforts.
- Speak at high school commencement or baccalaureate exercises.
- Give the invocation at high school events if this is allowed.
- Serve as mentor or big brother/big sister.
- Join the chamber of commerce and attend luncheons.
- Meet with the local clergy association.
- Volunteer at the local food pantry.

It is important to consider first the areas where your parishioners are already involved. For example, if you have a parishioner who is a member of the local school board, they can likely get you an invitation to speak at a baccalaureate ceremony or as a motivational speaker at a teacher in-service day. They can gain you entrance into organizations where you might not otherwise be invited.

Increasing Your Church's Involvement in the Community

Many churches engage in social outreach ministries in their local communities. This is both important and laudable, but there is more to community involvement than social outreach ministries. The more touches that parishioners can have through activities that are clearly identified as being from the church, the more doors into the church the community will find.

- All the news that's fit to print. Get to know your local newspaper editor or religion editor. Provide your local newspaper with news articles. At my last church, we asked at every staff meeting what articles we might submit to the local newspaper. You may not get them all published, but you'll probably get more published than you get now. Pay for advertising from time to time so you don't come across as a freeloader.
- I love a parade. Build a float and put it in your community's local parade—not once but several years in a row. This will heighten your church's name identity.
- Tax stamp giveaway. I know of one church that gave away postage stamps at their local post office on April 15. They gave away 500 stamps on a little card that said "Feeling Taxed? Here's a small gift to relieve the stress and let you know God loves you—no strings attached" with their church's name and address.

- Community Easter egg hunt. Hold this not at the church but in a public park. Be careful with this, the church might have more people show up than it can handle. If you are ill-prepared and have too many children show up with not enough eggs or volunteers, the church could actually get a worse reputation than if you had done nothing at all.
- Block party. Hold a neighborhood block party or festival with booths, music, and food for the neighborhood children.
- Health fair. Hold a health fair at your church. Provide for blood pressure, cholesterol checks, simple eye exams, and so forth.
- Praise in the park. Provide bright Christian music on a high-traffic day at a local park. Provide refreshments.
- Commercial spots. Sometimes local television cable providers will allow free commercial time to churches. Episcopal Radio and Television Foundation has some top-quality TV spots. Contact your local cable operator to see if they will run your ads free of cost.
- This is just the beginning of what can be done. Consider yourself a missionary in your community. Who are the people not connected with a local church? Where do they gather? What are their interests? Their needs?

***Quick Insight**: Stop at a local gas station or coffee shop and ask for directions to your church. You will find out fairly quickly how high is the church's profile in the community.*

Your Church's Web Site

Does your church have a Web site? You say you can't afford it? You can't afford *not* to have a Web site. Sixty-five percent of American adults claim to have Internet access. How a church can say it wants to bring new people into the church and not have a Web site is incomprehensible.

However, you must count the cost. Don't launch a Web site that you don't keep up-to-date. There is nothing worse than a Web site with news that hasn't been updated in 4 months. (I recently checked out a church's Web site that had listed their vicar—with picture—a priest that hadn't been there for several years!) It's better to have only a one-pane informational page that doesn't change than to have outdated information.

You don't have to have a state-of-the art-with-all-the-bells-and-whistles Web site. Too many "bells and whistles" may slow down the download time. Yes, people want attractiveness and creativity, but they also like their information to be instant. Too long of a download time, and you'll lose your surfers.

Consider hiring one of the youths in your church as your Webmaster. The chances are pretty good that you have someone who could do this easily as a part-time job—remember, this generation grew up with computers.

Actually, you don't even have to have a custom-designed Web site. There are businesses that have "canned" Web sites for which you pick your design, the features you need, insert your church's logo, and you have a state-of-the-art Web site with very little investment and very easy upkeep.

***Closer Look**: You say that your church can't afford to have a Web site designed, hosted, and kept up? Consider this: Let's say it costs $1,200 to have a Web site designed for your church; $75 per year for Web hosting; and $2,400 per year to have a youth keep up your Web site. If your Web site brings in one new family with a $2,000 pledge, you will have recouped your investment within two years.*

When designing your Web site, ask yourself, "Who is your customer, and what does your customer consider value?" In other words, what are people looking for when they access your church's Web site? There are generally three kinds of people you want to target:

People Checking Out Your Church

Yes, people do shop for a church online. They are looking for a "virtual experience" of your church before they ever walk in the door. It is helpful to have sample music, sample sermons, pictures of staff and key volunteers, and pictures of the church community gathered to give newcomers a clue about how they should expect to dress if they attend your church.

People Wanting to Be More Involved

There are some people who already attend your church that want to know how to connect at a deeper level. They want to know what sorts of classes, groups, program offerings, and ministries that they can connect with.

Members Who Need Information

Some of your members are looking for news or information on events that they know about or have heard about.

Before you design your own Web site, check out the Web sites of a couple of churches that are a little larger than yours. What's good about them? Where are there shortcomings? How much "flash" is too much?

***Closer Look**: Go ahead. Stop right now and check out the information on your Web site? Is all the information current? Is the design something to be proud of? How user-friendly is it? What does it say about your church?*

Turning Shoppers into Visitors

Most people visit a church because they are invited. Still, there are people who are looking for a church who may not know any of your parishioners. You might call these folks church shoppers. They're not yet visitors, but they're checking out your church without your knowing it. Some of these church shoppers never visited, and you never got the opportunity to be a warm and friendly church because what they saw before Sunday morning made them decide not to give you a try. In Chapter 11, we dealt with improving the church's facilities. This section asks the church leader to look at the building through the eye of the person who is not yet a visitor, the person who hasn't yet decided whether to visit. Consider the following four ways that the interested-but-casual church shopper will likely interface with your church.

Curb Appeal

What is the "curb appeal" of your church? Try this: drive by your church at 5 miles per hour. If you were a visitor, would you want to visit your church? Is your church well kept? Inviting? Are there piles of clutter? How about your lawn and flower beds? What shape is your parking lot in? Is your front entrance obvious? How about the church sign?

Church Sign

Refer to the discussion in Chapter 11. Would a complete stranger understand the difference between "Rite I" and "Rite II?" How about simply calling it a "worship service?" Research indicates that 10 percent of your new members will come because of the church sign.

Spec Sheet

Note the discussion in Chapter 11 about placing a Plexiglas magazine rack to provide information on the church for the drive-by shopper.

Answering Machine

Have you checked your answering machine message lately? Are you still announcing your Christmas Eve services? Most people respond more favorably to a female voice on an answering machine than a male voice. On Sunday mornings, have a live person answering the church telephone. A live person can be a friendly voice to the newcomer, give directions in case people get lost, connect with worshippers in case of emergency, and, oh, yes, tell folks if the bishop is going to be late because of traffic.

Welcoming Newcomers

And now, here are a few suggestions for welcoming newcomers:

Greeters

Have greeters that can truly greet people. If you're depending on your ushers to be the primary greeters, you are probably overloading them. You want to have people feel like they have time to greet people. If they have the time, they will give the time.

Newcomer's or Information Table or Booth

Some people will actually want to be able to get information about how they can connect with the church. Have the church's informational resources available here, such as newsletters, parish directory, brochures on baptisms and weddings, and so on. Also, have someone at the front of the table to greet people as well.

Welcome Bag

Many churches are giving out gift bags to newcomers as a way of making them feel welcome and giving them information regarding the church. The question to ask when assembling a newcomer's gift bag is: what are we trying to communicate? How you answer this question will generally depend on the size of your congregation.

A church with Sunday attendance of 120 or less will want to communicate that the church is primarily a warm, friendly, and caring church. The people who would typically be attracted to a church of this size would want to know whether this is a warm and caring fellowship and whether there is a place for them. People who would be attracted to this size of church ask questions such as, "Do I fit here? Are this church's values compatible with mine?" If your Sunday attendance is 120 or more, your church's overarching purpose is to connect people to a ministry or program offering in the church.

Here are some suggestions for a newcomer's bag:

- Monthly newsletter.
- What is Anglicanism?
- Frequently asked questions (FAQs) on worship (liturgy).
- Children's offerings.
- Nursery guidelines.
- List of small-group offerings or Bible studies, men's or women's groups, and so forth.
- Mission and outreach opportunities.
- CD of music and preaching excerpts.
- Pocket cross with a card on how to use it.
- Coupon to redeem for gift at newcomer's table or information booth (it's even better if your priest, staff member, or lay person has written a book).

Welcome Letter

Consider sending your visitors a welcome letter from the rector along with a short survey (on a stamped, self-addressed post card) that they would mail back to the church office. This card would ask basic info, along with feedback on their experience, such as did the ushers greet them, how were the nursery facilities, did they experience a sense of worship, how might the church improve for the visitor, and so on. In appreciation for completing the survey, include a token to be redeemed for a gift at the newcomer's table.

Suggestions for Individuals Who Want to Develop a Welcoming Congregation

Many growing congregations grow, not because they have a particularly excellent newcomer's ministry, but because they are a welcoming congregation. Although it certainly helps to have a quality newcomer's ministry, many congregations grow because they are, quite simply, welcoming congregations. They are aware of the newcomers in their midst, and they have a value of "welcoming the stranger."

***Closer Look**: Ask a friend to visit your church and tell you how friendly and welcoming the people in your church are. Ask them to do this as a favor to you. (Be careful; they might end up staying.)*

These suggestions for becoming a welcoming congregation are not so much programmatic as they are values that individuals can embrace. Here are seven:

1. Remember the rule of 3 to 1. (Thanks to St. Nicholas, Flower Mound, Texas, for this suggestion.) The rule of 3 to 1 is this: talk to three newcomers on any given Sunday for every one regular person that you talk to. Remember that church is for fellowship as well as business and that busy leaders should avoid the impulse to spend times of fellowship doing business with other busy leaders

2. Pass off the new person you've just met to someone else. Don't just greet someone and say, "It was nice to meet you." Introduce them to someone else. Let your newcomers connect to as many people as possible.

3. Introduce yourself with a question. Many people don't like to talk to newcomers because they are afraid of embarrassing themselves by mistaking a long-time member with a newcomer. An easy way to get around that fear is to introduce yourself, "Hi, my name is ______. I've been coming here two years. How long have you been coming to this church?" This open-ended question doesn't presume that the person you're speaking with is a newcomer or a member. It allows them to reveal either.

4. Don't monopolize the priest. Most newcomers really would like to visit with the priest. I once visited a church where the line to talk to both priests was about 25 people long. So, I left rather than wait to visit with the priests. They need to be available to greet the new folks. The priest is one of the greatest evangelistic tools that the church has.

5. When giving directions: take, don't point. When I go to my local sporting goods store, I'm always so impressed that when I ask for directions, the customer service agent never points me in the direction where I need to go. This person usually walks with me until we get to the department that I'm looking for. In most of our churches, this kind of personal assistance only takes a minute. Don't point them in the direction of the nursery, take them there. It is so gracious. (Besides, my mother always told me that it is not polite to point.)

6. Have a positive attitude about your church. If you're not excited about your church, nobody else will be, either. A positive attitude is infectious.

7. Don't just meet, invite. That is, don't just say hello to the newcomer, find out what his or her interests are and connect that person with an appropriate activity or person in the church, such as ministry, small group, Sunday school class, Bible study, and so forth.

Chapter 15

Reaching Beyond Your Church by Using Missions and Outreach as a Catalyst for Growth

. . . . in Jerusalem, and in all Judea and Samaria, and to the ends of the earth.

—Acts 1:8

Being a missionary is at the heart of who God is. At the point of humanity's need, God sent His Son to save the world. Having made us in His image, God has placed that missionary impetus in our souls as well. We were born to be sent, born to engage in mission and outreach. We must be involved in a purpose larger than ourselves. If we do not engage in mission at some level, a part of our soul dies.

The church also was made to be missionary. "The Church," wrote Archbishop William Temple famously, "is the only institution in the world that exists for the benefit of those who are not yet its members." Elsewhere he would write (with even more passion) that a "church that lives for itself dies by itself!"

If a church is not actively involved in outreach and missions, a part of its corporate soul is impaired, and the members of the congregation have a sense of unease because they instinctively know that the church is not really fulfilling its purpose for being.

Growing Churches Are Reaching-Out Churches

A Fuller Theological Seminary study of growing churches found that growth occurred in local congregations whenever at least 15 percent of its active membership was involved in ministry of any kind to people outside their congregation. Surprisingly, the nature of that outreach ministry—whether it was social outreach programs such as soup kitchens or ministries specifically intended to bring in new members—appeared not to matter. The one common denominator among congregations that grew was that a significant percentage of their community was willing to reach out beyond themselves.

It did not matter whether the people were involved in evangelism, or social outreach ministries, or missions: the two relevant factors were that, one, the ministry was aimed at people outside the congregation; and two, at least 15 percent of the active members were involved in such ministries.

Reaching-Out Churches Attract People Who Need Reaching Out To

Is it really all that surprising in the final analysis that extroverted parishes grow and introverted parishes don't? Church-shopping outsiders who want to become insiders are much more likely to try out a parish if they already have crossed paths with the work of that parish in the larger community. A church that exists for itself is neither being faithful to the Gospel nor is attractive to newcomers. Imagine a young couple waking up on a Saturday morning after a long night out partying the night before. They have decided to find a church where their soon-to-be family can get involved so they can raise their children with good spiritual values. As they are discussing which churches to visit, I doubt that they will say to each other, "Let's visit a church that is self-absorbed. We don't really want a church where they look much beyond themselves and don't have a hard time getting Sunday school teachers because we just want pastoral care and good worship."

No, people who are looking for a church will first look for those churches that have a reputation for caring and reaching beyond themselves. As we stated above, God has implanted in our souls a motivation to reach beyond ourselves. People looking for a church will instinctively look for a church that is corporately fulfilling that God-given desire. They may not initially want to be involved themselves, but they want to be a part of a church that is doing so. Whether they articulate it or not, they know that that is what churches are supposed to do. They will be drawn to a purpose-fulfilling church. The task of discipleship is to move them from a place of wanting to be a part of a church that is involved in missions and outreach to where they are themselves involved in the mission and outreach of the church.

Increasing Missions and Outreach

Outreach of any kind has a powerful, galvanizing effect upon the congregation. Once a congregation is connected to this power—whether through social activism programs or evangelism—the natural impulse is to press on, to go further, and still further. To do otherwise is detrimental—financially and, more importantly, spiritually.

Here's a bit more to the story of the church in Chapter 5 that had reduced the missions and outreach portion of their budget. Recall that this action had a devastating effect on the morale of the church. A fuller telling of the story includes the foreign missions component.

In the second year of the rector's tenure, they were ready to increase their financial commitment to missions and outreach. They recruited people for short-term mission trips to Honduras and to Russia; they partnered with two other congregations to help plant a church in Honduras and committed to working and supporting the congregation there for at least five years. The rector served on the board of a local outreach agency and on the pastoral steering committee to respond to a local community disaster.

Perhaps even more significantly, they were ready to commit five percent of their operating budget to outreach. They agreed that we would contribute only to those ministries in which parishioners were already actively involved. In this way, even though we started with a small amount of money, there was an incarnational connection between our money and our members. Our church began to be perceived by its members and by the larger community as being a healthy church, taking care of its own people, who in turn were then able and willing to take care of others. There were some dramatic net results of this shifted perception. Within a space of three years, income was up and our average Sunday attendance increased by more than 33 percent.

Two Foundational Underpinnings

Many churches simply do missions and outreach because "that's what churches are supposed to do." Although that may be a good motivation for being involved in missions and outreach, your church can get much more than personal satisfaction if you do it the right way, that is, if it's a healthy part of the church. Before exploring how to raise the profile of missions and outreach in your church, let's discuss two foundational underpinnings that are crucial if you want to use missions and outreach to develop a healthy congregation.

Don't forget these two phrases:

- Incarnational connection
- Right-sized

Incarnational Connection

The first value for missions and outreach support in the local church is that there must be an incarnational connection with the ministry being supported. This is a theological way of saying that people in the church ought to be involved in the ministry before the church contributes any money to that ministry. Why?

The church supports people involved in missions and outreach ministry because it is an effective way to form its own disciples. If the choice is between supporting a ministry where parishioners are involved and supporting one where there are no parishioners, of course we would support the parishioner-connected ministry! Then it becomes "our" ministry.

Right-Sized

Second, the missions and outreach involvement must be "right-sized" for its church size.

Lion tamers say that the reason a lion tamer will go into a lion's cage with only a whip and a stool is that the lion gets confused by the four legs of the stool and doesn't know which leg to concentrate on. Similarly, smaller churches that support too many ministries end up confusing their parishioners by not sending a clear signal about "what the church is really about." A small church that supports only one or two ministries gives the church a clearer identity about its priorities and a more unified witness to both the community and its own parishioners. As the church grows to the transitional size and beyond, it can begin to expand those external ministries in a way more appropriate to its size. It is much better to do one or two things well than several things with mediocrity or inadequate support.

Ways to Raise the Missions and Outreach Profile of Your Church

When it comes to raising the missions and outreach profile of the church, remember that there are two target audiences: the congregation and the public. Communicating the missions and outreach involvement of the church to the congregation itself communicates to the congregation as a whole that the church is fulfilling its purpose, namely, to extend the church's arms of love to the poor and needy and to those who need the gospel. Ultimately, this raises the congregation's self-esteem and makes the church a more attractive community of faith to invite their friends and acquaintances to. Here are some ways to communicate within the parish:

- Place a monthly article in the parish newsletter on an outreach ministry or mission opportunity that the church is involved in.
- Place a short paragraph in the weekly worship leaflet.
- Mention the outreach ministry or mission trip in the prayers of the people with a specific prayer request (i.e., don't simply "file by category").
- Conduct a 5-minute interview with a parishioner who is involved in a specific ministry or who has just returned from a mission trip.
- During the church service immediately before they leave, pray for those going on their short-term mission trip.
- Dedicate bulletin board space with a map of the world and show the places where the church has sent short-term missionaries or supports missionaries.
- Do the same with a map of the church's city or town, highlighting the outreach ministries that parishioners are involved in or the church supports.
- Print thank you notes or letters received from recipients of the church's mission or outreach efforts.

The second target for communicating the missional and outreach involvement of the church is the surrounding community itself. As the local church becomes known as a church that cares for the local community and offshore missions, the church will itself become a magnet for those who are aiming to make a difference in other people's lives.

Here are some suggestions for raising the missions and outreach profile of your church:

- Have a missions-emphasis Sunday on a regular basis and invite a missionary to preach. Be sure to have this event published in the local newspaper.
- Write an article on the church's short-term missions trip or outreach ministry—with photos—for the local newspaper.
- Invite a short-term mission group from another church to recruit members from your church—with the aim that your church will develop its own team within two years. Again, write an article for the local newspaper.
- Sponsor a community involvement day in which your church recruits parishioners to assist local helping ministries with 4- to 6-hour volunteers to assist with their local ministries. One church that I know of calls this a "Make a Difference Day."

Ultimately, the crucial thing to remember in highlighting your church's concern for others is not so much to give great sums of money to other people's ministries but to give people to those ministries. Then, let the church's financial resources follow where the people are involved.

Notes

1. Arlin Rothauge, *Sizing Up the Congregation* (Episcopal Church Center, 1982).
2. Carl S. Dudley, *Making the Small Church Effective* (Nashville: Abingdon, 1978).
3. Charles Handy, *The Age of Paradox* (Boston: Harvard Press, 1994), 55.
4. Rothauge, *Reshaping a Congregation for a New Future* (Episcopal Church Center, 1985), 15–20.
5. James MacGregor Burns, *Leadership* (New York: Harper & Row, 1978).
6. Max DePree, *Leadership is an Art* (New York: Dell, 1989), 11.
7. John Maxwell, *Developing the Leader Within You* (Nashville: Thomas Nelson Publishers, 1993), 5.
8. Ibid.
9. Henri J. M. Nouwen, *The Wounded Healer* (Garden City, NY: Image Books, 1979), 39.
10. Mission status meant that the congregation received financial assistance from the diocese. Parish status meant that the congregation was financially self-sufficient and could afford a full-time priest serving in residence.
11. Nouwen, "Moving from Solitude to Community to Ministry," *Leadership Journal*, vol. 16, No. 2 (Spring 1995).
12. Paul Braoudakis, *Willow Creek Community Church Leaders Handbook*, 3rd ed. (Barrington, IL: Willow Creek Assoc., 1996), 70; Rick Warren, *The Purpose Driven Church* (Grand Rapids: Zondervan, 1995), 144.
13. Jim Collins, *Good to Great* (New York: Harper Business, 2001).
14. http://www.episcopalchurch.org/documents/CDR_FACTSummary.pdf
15. Loren Meade, *Five Challenges for the Once and Future Church*, (Bethesda, MD: Alban Institute, 1996)
16. Ibid., 36.

17. Ibid., 38–39.
18. Ibid., 39.
19. Ibid.
20. Ibid., 40.
21. Ibid., 40–42.
22. Rudolf Otto, *The Idea of the Holy* (London: Oxford University Press, 1958).
23. Robert Webber, *Ancient-Future Faith* (Grand Rapids: Baker Books, 1999); and Webber, *Ancient-Future Evangelism* (Grand Rapids: Baker Books, 2003).
24. Dan Kimball, *The Emerging Church* (Grand Rapids: Zondervan, 2003) and Kimball, *Emerging Worship* (Grand Rapids: Zondervan, 2004).
25. Charles Bartow, *Effective Speech Communication in Leading Worship* (Nashville: Abingdon, 1988).
26. Ibid., 71.
27. Ibid., 117.
28. Lyle Schaller, *44 Ways to Increase Church Attendance* (Nashville: Abingdon, 1988), 21.
29. Ibid., 44.
30. Murray Frick, *Reach the Back Row* (Loveland, CO: Vital Ministry, 1999), 13–18.
31. Ibid., 21 ff.
32. Ibid., p. 22.